NATIONALITY, IMMIGRATION AND ASYLUM ACT

EXPLANATORY NOTES

INTRODUCTION

1.   These explanatory notes relate to the Nationality, Immigration and Asylum Act, which received Royal Assent on 7 November 2002. They have been prepared by the Home Office in order to assist the reader in understanding the Act. They do not form part of the Act and have not been endorsed by Parliament.

2.   The notes need to be read in conjunction with the Act. They are not, and are not meant to be, a comprehensive description of the Act. So where a section or part of a section does not seem to require any explanation or comment, none is given.

OVERVIEW

3.   The Act is in eight parts:

- Part 1 contains provisions which amend British nationality legislation, primarily the British Nationality Act 1981 ("BNA 1981"). It includes provision for citizenship ceremonies and a pledge, and imposes a requirement for naturalisation as a British citizen that the applicant has sufficient knowledge about life in the United Kingdom;

- Part 2 contains provisions for the support of asylum-seekers in accommodation centres, built or adapted to accommodate and provide services for a number of asylum-seekers and their dependants on one site;

- Part 3 concerns support arrangements for asylum-seekers and other assistance;

- Part 4 contains provisions relating to detention, temporary release and removal;

- Part 5 contains provisions on immigration and asylum appeals;

- Part 6 contains provisions relating to immigration procedures, including charges for work permits, establishment of an Authority-to-carry scheme, and the provision of information and disclosure;

- Part 7 introduces new offences and powers of entry to business premises; and

- Part 8 contains general provisions.

SUMMARY

Part 1 - Nationality

4.   The provisions:

- Introduce citizenship ceremonies and a citizenship pledge;

- Require those who apply for naturalisation as a British citizen to have sufficient knowledge about life in the United Kingdom; allow for regulations to be made which would specify how this requirement – and the existing requirement in relation to knowledge of English, Welsh or Scottish Gaelic – is to be met; extend the language requirement to those applying for naturalisation as the spouse of a British citizen or a British overseas territories citizen;

- Amend the grounds for deprivation of citizenship, and replace the existing procedure for reviewing the deprivation decision with a new right of appeal against deprivation;

- Remove existing provisions which allow discrimination on the grounds of nationality or ethnic or national origin in the exercise of nationality functions;

- Remove the present distinctions in nationality law between legitimate and illegitimate children;

- Repeal both the present statutory exemptions from the duty to give reasons for nationality decisions and the provisions which restrict the court's ability to review certain decisions. Other nationality provisions which are now spent are also repealed;

- Remove the minimum age requirement for applications for registration as a British citizen or a British overseas territories citizen by stateless children born in the United Kingdom and the British overseas territories;

- Clarify the meaning of the expression "in the United Kingdom in breach of the immigration laws", where it occurs in the BNA 1981;

- Enable men as well as women who renounced British nationality before 1983, and who now wish to re-gain it, to rely on a marital connection with the United Kingdom or a British overseas territory;

- Enable regulation of the procedure for applying for a certificate of entitlement to the right of abode in the United Kingdom;

- Confer an entitlement to registration as a British citizen on certain British Overseas citizens, British subjects and British protected persons; and

- Confer a similar entitlement on certain persons who, but for gender discrimination in the law in force before 1 January 1983, would have acquired British citizenship automatically on that date.

Part 2 - Accommodation Centres

5.   Part 2 of the Act makes provision for the introduction of accommodation centres, built or adapted to accommodate and provide services for a number of asylum-seekers and their dependants on one site. The centres will be introduced on a trial basis. A proportion of new asylum-seekers who request, and are eligible for, support will be offered places in accommodation centres. Those who refuse the offer of a place, voluntarily cease to reside in a centre or breach their conditions of residence will not qualify for other forms of support. The centres may provide for a number of facilities and services, including:

- Food and other essential items;

- Money;

- Assistance with transport and assistance with expenses to pursue purposeful activities;

- Facilities for religious observance;

- Healthcare; and

- Education and training.

Part 3 - Other Support and Assistance

6.   The new asylum system will be based on a network of induction, accommodation and reporting centres as well as existing National Asylum Support Service ("NASS") accommodation. Part 3 of the Act enables reporting and residence requirements to be imposed on all asylum-seekers and allows for the discontinuation of support to asylum-seekers who fail without reasonable cause to report as required. The Act also includes a number of provisions about the way in which those in the asylum system are supported. It also includes a provision for the Secretary of State to make payments

to local authorities and voluntary organisations to reimburse them for the support they have provided for Unaccompanied Asylum Seeking Children ("UASCs"). This does not affect the amount paid to local authorities.

7. Part 3 of the Act also contains provisions making certain categories of person ineligible for support unless provision is made in regulations to the contrary. Examples include those who have refugee status in another EU Member State and persons unlawfully in the UK. Part 3 additionally prohibits, subject to certain exceptions, the provision of support to asylum seekers who fail to make their asylum claim as soon as reasonably practicable after their arrival in the UK.

8. This Part of the Act also contains provision enabling funding of a voluntary assisted return programme ("VARP") and international projects. The VARP is a means by which assistance is provided to asylum-seekers who wish to return home. The current VARP scheme is administered for the Home Office by the International Organisation for Migration in partnership with Refugee Action. Examples of international projects that may be funded under the power include resettlement and the "interception assisted return programmes". The power would allow funding of a United Kingdom resettlement programme which would allow a scheme to be established whereby those who cannot be protected in their region of origin may be entitled to have their claim for protection considered before they reach the United Kingdom, and enable the cost of their travel and settlement here to be met. Any resettlement programme would operate in addition to the current asylum determination procedures. This provision also enables the Secretary of State to participate in research projects relating to migration, and fund organisations and bodies that are involved in such projects.

Part 4 - Detention and Removal

9. Part 4 of the Act contains a number of measures designed to simplify the process of removing those who have no right to stay in the United Kingdom. These include:

- Giving detainee custody officers acting as escorts a limited power to enter private premises to search persons being taken into detention;

- Giving the Secretary of State power to detain where he has power to give or refuse leave to enter, or where he has power to set removal directions, and giving the Secretary of State a power to grant bail equivalent to the power of immigration officers;

- The power to remove children born in the United Kingdom, where their parents entered the United Kingdom unlawfully; and

- The power to remove those who attempt to obtain permission to stay by using deception.

10. This Part also contains a provision allowing a residence restriction to be imposed on an asylum-seeker requiring him to reside for up to 14 days at a specified location at or

near a place where an induction programme is to be made available to him. In addition a provision has been included which creates a rebuttable presumption that someone who has been convicted of a crime and given a custodial sentence of two years or more or an offence specified by order has been convicted of a particularly serious crime and is a danger to the community for the purposes of Article 33(2) of the Refugee Convention and accordingly cannot rely on that Convention to prevent their removal.

Part 5 - Appeals

11. The Immigration and Asylum Act 1999 ("the 1999 Act") introduced a one-stop appeal requiring an adjudicator considering an immigration appeal to deal with any other appealable matters raised by the applicant at the same time. The provisions in Part 5 of the Act aim to re-structure the appeals system and will:

- Define the specific immigration decisions which attract a right of appeal;

- Provide for asylum or human rights claims to be certified where the claim is clearly unfounded or where the person is to be removed to a country of which they are not a national and the Secretary of State has no reason to believe that their rights under the ECHR will be breached in that country. The effect of such certification is that the person cannot, other than in limited cases, appeal against the immigration decision while in the United Kingdom;

- Enable the certification of applications, preventing a further right of appeal where a person could have made the application earlier or raised it at an earlier appeal but did not do so;

- Introduce a statutory review process as an alternative remedy to judicial review for challenges to the Immigration Appeal Tribunal decision to refuse permission to appeal;

- Enable rules to provide a statutory closure date to prevent multiple adjournments of cases at the adjudicator stage; and

- Enable rules to provide wasted cost powers and a 'no merit' certificate which can be issued by the Immigration Appellate Authority.

Part 6 - Immigration Procedure

12. Part 6 of the Act contains provisions that allow a fee to be set for work permit applications, and bring work permit advice within the remit of the Office of the Immigration Services Commissioner.

13. The Act also contains provisions to introduce a scheme to require physical data, such as iris or facial images, to accompany applications to enter or remain in the United Kingdom. The Secretary of State may also operate a scheme to allow people voluntarily to provide such data to assist their entry into the United Kingdom. There is

also provision which allows the introduction of an Authority- to-carry ("ATC") scheme. This provides for regulations to require carriers to check the details of passengers against a Home Office database to confirm that they pose no known immigration or security risk.

14. The Secretary of State will also be able to require an employer, financial institution, or local authority to supply him with specified information. The Inland Revenue will be able to supply specified information to the Secretary of State for certain purposes, and port medical inspectors and staff working under their direction will be able to disclose information to specified health service bodies where necessary for certain medical purposes. The disclosure gateway at section 20 of the 1999 Act is also extended.

15. This Part also introduces Schedule 8, which amends the existing carriers' liability provisions in Part II of the 1999 Act. This establishes a more flexible penalty regime, introduces a statutory right of appeal and modifies the provisions for the detention of transporters. The provisions also apply to the rail freight regime (section 39 of the 1999 Act) and the carriers' liability regime (sections 40 to 42 of the 1999 Act).

16. Part 6 also includes provision for a power that would allow the UK to operate immigration and other frontier controls at an European Economic Area sea port such as Calais, subject to an international agreement. In addition, it would allow the Secretary of State to make any necessary legislative arrangements to accommodate French immigration control in UK Channel ports such as Dover.

Part 7 - Offences

17. Part 7 of the Act includes new criminal offences of: assisting unlawful immigration; trafficking of people into, out of or within the UK for the purpose of prostitution; forgery and similar activities relating to the Application Registration Card; failure to comply with a notice requesting information in respect of suspected immigration offending; and an offence relating to the possession of an immigration stamp, whether genuine or a replica, without a reasonable excuse. This part also amends and modifies the law on offences relating to the employment of persons who are subject to immigration control; This Part also contains provisions which give police and immigration officers the power to enter business premises to search for and arrest immigration offenders, and to inspect and seize personnel records following the arrest of an immigration offender on those premises.

COMMENTARY ON SECTIONS

PART 1: NATIONALITY

Section 1: Naturalisation: knowledge of language and society

18. Section 1 amends the provisions in the BNA 1981 which set out the requirements that an applicant for naturalisation as a British citizen must satisfy. (There is already a requirement, in paragraph 1(1)(c) of Schedule 1 to the BNA 1981, for certain

applicants to have a sufficient knowledge of English, Welsh or Scottish Gaelic.)

19.   Subsection (1) adds to Schedule 1 of the BNA 1981 a requirement for the applicant to demonstrate sufficient knowledge about life in the United Kingdom.

20.   Subsection (2) enables the Secretary of State to waive the requirement that an applicant must have sufficient knowledge about life in the United Kingdom where he considers that, because of the applicant's age or physical or mental condition, it would be unreasonable to expect him or her to fulfil it.

21.   Subsection (3) enables provision to be made by regulations for determining whether a person has a sufficient knowledge of a language and whether a person has sufficient knowledge about life in the United Kingdom for the purpose of an application for naturalisation.

22.   By subsection (4) the regulations may make provision about how those requirements of sufficient knowledge of language and about life in the United Kingdom are met (for example, by reference to a specified qualification or attendance on a specified course).

Section 2: Naturalisation: spouse of citizen

23.   Section 2 extends the requirement to have sufficient knowledge of a relevant language to those applying for naturalisation on the basis of marriage to a British citizen or a British overseas territories citizen. This section also requires those applying for naturalisation on the basis of marriage to a British citizen to have sufficient knowledge about life in the United Kingdom.

Section 3: Citizenship ceremony, oath and pledge

24.   Section 3 introduces Schedule 1, which amends the current provisions in the BNA 1981 about naturalisation and registration procedure.

25.   Paragraph 1 of Schedule 1 replaces section 42 of the BNA 1981 with provision requiring persons, except minors, who are naturalised or registered as British citizens, to attend citizenship ceremonies and make a citizenship pledge as well as the existing oath. It also extends to applicants for British overseas territories citizenship the requirement to make a pledge. The Secretary of State is given a discretion to disapply these requirements in particular cases.

26.   Paragraph 2 of Schedule 1 replaces Schedule 5 to the BNA 1981. It introduces a new "citizenship oath and pledge" which is to be taken by applicants for registration or naturalisation as British citizens and British overseas territories citizens. The citizenship oath and pledge consists of the existing oath of allegiance with the addition of a pledge. The pledge for those becoming British citizens states that the person will respect the rights and freedoms of the United Kingdom, and will uphold its democratic values, observe its laws and fulfil the duties and obligations of citizenship. Applicants becoming British overseas territories citizens will instead

pledge loyalty to the relevant British overseas territory.

27.   Paragraph 4 of Schedule 1 amends the existing regulation-making power in subsection 41(1)(d) of the BNA 1981 to enable regulation of the timing of attendance at a citizenship ceremony and the taking of the citizenship oath and pledge, the content and conduct of the citizenship ceremony, the completion and grant of a certificate of registration or naturalisation, and certain other related matters.

28.   Paragraph 7 of Schedule 1 enables the Secretary of State to make regulations about the persons who shall be authorised to conduct citizenship ceremonies and to require local authorities in England, Wales and Scotland to provide facilities for the conduct of such ceremonies.

29.   Paragraph 8 allows the Secretary of State to reimburse local authorities for the cost of carrying out citizenship ceremonies.

Section 4: Deprivation of citizenship

30.   Section 4 makes new provision about the deprivation of British nationality or status.

31.   Subsection (1) replaces existing section 40 of the BNA 1981 and inserts a new section 40A.

32.   New section 40(1) of the BNA 1981 lists the categories of persons who are liable to deprivation under the Act. These are British citizens, British overseas territories citizens, British Overseas citizens, British Nationals (Overseas), British subjects and British protected persons.

33.   New section 40(2) provides that a person may be deprived of his citizenship status if he has done anything seriously prejudicial to the vital interests of the United Kingdom or a British overseas territory.

34.   New section 40(3) provides that a person may be deprived of his citizenship status if the registration or naturalisation by virtue of which the status was acquired was obtained by means of fraud, false representation or by concealment of a material fact.

35.   New section 40(4) provides that a person may not be deprived of their citizenship status on the ground mentioned in subsection (2) if this would make him stateless.

36.   New section 40(5) provides that before making a deprivation order the Secretary of State must give the person written notice specifying that a decision has been made to make the order and the reasons for it. The notice must also advise the person of his right to appeal.

37.   New section 40(6) repeats the provision made by subsection (3) in respect of fraudulently obtained registrations and naturalisations effected or granted before

1983.

38.   New section 40A confers a right of appeal to an adjudicator (in the first instance)on a person in respect of whom a decision to deprive him of his citizenship status has been made. There is also provision for both parties to appeal to the Tribunal from the adjudicator on a point of law. From the Tribunal there is a further appeal, again on a point of law, to the Court of Appeal, or the Court of Session (if the adjudicator's decision was in Scotland). Where, however, the Secretary of State has certified that the decision to deprive was based wholly or partly in reliance on information which he believes should not be made public for one of the reasons specified in new section 40A(2), the appeal at first instance will instead be heard by the Special Immigration Appeals Commission. New section 40A(6) prevents the making of an order under section 40 at any time when an appeal against this is pending, or could be brought, under section 40A or under section 2B of the Special Immigration Appeals Commission Act 1997 ("SIAC 1997").

39.   Subsections (2) and (3) make consequential amendments to SIAC 1997.

40.   Subsection (4) makes it clear that, in deciding whether there were grounds for deprivation under new section 40 of the 1981 Act, the Secretary of State would be entitled to have regard to events occurring <u>before</u> the commencement of that section <u>if</u> those events would have justified deprivation under section 40 of the Act as then in force.

Section 5: Resumption of citizenship
41.   Section 5 removes the words "if a woman" from sections 10 and 22 of the BNA 1981, thus allowing either a woman or a man who renounced their United Kingdom and Colonies citizenship before 1983 to qualify for registration on the basis of a connection with the United Kingdom (or a British overseas territory) through marriage.

Section 6: Nationality decision: discrimination
42.   Section 6 repeals the exemption from the general prohibition on discrimination in section 19B of the Race Relations Act 1976 ("the 1976 Act")(as amended by the Race Relations (Amendment) Act 2000), in so far as it applies to discrimination on the grounds of nationality, ethnic or national origins in the exercise of nationality functions. The "nationality functions" are functions exercisable by virtue of the BNA 1981, the British Nationality (Falkland Islands) Act 1983, the British Nationality (Hong Kong) Act 1990, the Hong Kong (War Wives and Widows) Act 1996 and the British Nationality (Hong Kong) Act 1997.

43.   Subsection (2) removes "nationality functions" from the scope of the exemption in subsection 19D(1) of the 1976 Act.

44.   Subsection (3) inserts into section 19D of the 1976 Act new definitions of "immigration functions" and "Immigration Acts", consequent upon the removal from

that section of references to nationality functions and statutes relating to nationality.

45.   Subsection (4) removes references to nationality functions from provisions in section 19E of the 1976 Act relating to the review by the Race Monitor of the use of the exemptions from discrimination, since this is made redundant by the other provisions in this section.

46.   Subsection (5) adds a new subsection (1A) to section 71A of the 1976 Act, defining "immigration and nationality functions" for the purpose of that section. The effect is to maintain the present exemption from the duty, under section 71(1)(b) of the Act, to promote equality of opportunity in relation to the carrying out of such functions.

Section 7: Nationality decision: reasons and review
47.   Section 7 repeals the provisions in section 44(2) of the BNA 1981 and corresponding provision in section 1 of the British Nationality (Hong Kong) Act 1990 which exempt the Secretary of State from having to give reasons for granting or refusing applications under the BNA 1981, where these decisions are at his discretion, and which restrict the ability of the courts to review such decisions.

48.   This section also repeals section 44(3) of the BNA 1981 since this is made redundant by the other provisions in this section.

Section 8: Citizenship: registration
49.   Section 8 removes the minimum age restriction for applicants seeking to acquire British citizenship or British overseas territories citizenship by registration on the grounds that they were born stateless in either the United Kingdom or a British overseas territory.

Section 9: Legitimacy of child
50.   Section 9 removes from the nationality legislation the present distinctions between legitimate and illegitimate children and inserts a new definition of "father" into section 50 of the BNA 1981.

51.   Subsection (1) provides that, for the purposes of the BNA 1981, a child's mother is the woman who gives birth to the child. A child's "father" is (a) the husband at the time of the child's birth of the woman who gives birth to the child, (b) a person who falls to be treated as the child's father by virtue of section 28 of the Human Fertilisation and Embryology Act 1990 or (c) any person who satisfies prescribed requirements as to proof of paternity. The Secretary of State may set out in regulations how, in circumstances where proof is required, paternity must be proven.

52.   Subsection (2) amends section 3(6) of the BNA 1981 to allow registration as a British citizen of an illegitimate minor born outside the United Kingdom on the basis of a connection through his father as well as through his mother.

53.   Subsection (3) makes similar provision as subsection (2) but in respect of registration

10

as a British overseas territories citizen under section 17 of the BNA 1981.

54. Subsection (4) repeals section 47 of the BNA 1981. This enables an illegitimate child of a British citizen father to be legitimated by the subsequent marriage between his mother and father. In view of the prospective abolition of distinctions between the legitimate and the illegitimate in this context, section 47 will be redundant so far as children born after the appointed commencement date are concerned.

55. Subsection (5) amends paragraph 1(1)(b) of Schedule 2 to the BNA 1981, which provides that an illegitimate child born in the United Kingdom after 1st January 1983 whose parents hold different British nationality statuses under the BNA 1981, can only acquire the status of the mother. By this subsection, the position of illegitimate children is brought into line with that of legitimate children, who can acquire citizenship or status through either parent.

Section 10: Right of abode: certificate of entitlement

56. Section 10 enables regulations to be made in relation to the issue of a certificate of entitlement to the right of abode in the United Kingdom. The procedure is currently unregulated, except in regard to the level of fee and procedure for appealing against a refusal to issue such a certificate. A certificate of entitlement is currently defined as a certificate stating that a person has the right of abode in the United Kingdom. Section 2 of the Immigration 1971 Act ("the 1971 Act") sets out who has the right of abode.

57. Regulations are to be made by statutory instrument . The regulations may specify such matters as the person to whom the application must be made, the form of the application and the documents which are to accompany it. They may also make provision for certificates to be revoked in certain circumstances, for example, where obtained by the provision of false information, and for the certificate to cease to have effect after a specified time.

58. Subsection (5) defines "certificate of entitlement", for the purposes of the 1971 Act by reference to the new provision.

59. Subsection (6) enables regulations made under this section to preserve the effect of any certificate issued in accordance with the existing procedures.

Section 11: Unlawful presence in United Kingdom

60. Section 11 makes provision for construing the expression "in the United Kingdom in breach of the immigration laws" where it occurs in section 4 of, and Schedule 1 to, the BNA 1981 (registration and naturalisation) and in subsection 50(5) of that Act (meaning of "ordinary residence").

61. Subsection (2) provides that a person is "in the United Kingdom in breach of the immigration laws" at any time when he was here without leave or other entitlement, for example under Community law.

62.   Subsection (3) ensures that a person is *not* treated as being in the United Kingdom at any time when he had not "entered the United Kingdom" within the meaning of section 11 of the 1971 Act. (Section 11 provides that a person is deemed not to have entered the United Kingdom before disembarkation, while in a controlled area at a port or while under immigration control. This includes periods of detention and "temporary admission" under the 1971 Act.)

63.   Subsection (4) states that the provisions in this section should be treated as having always had effect, except in relation to certain European Economic Area nationals and their family members.

64.   Subsection (5) states that the rule of construction in subsection (2) is without prejudice to the meaning of "in breach of the immigration laws" where it occurs in other contexts.

Section 12:   British citizenship: registration of certain persons without other citizenship
65.   Section 12 inserts a new provision into the BNA 1981, conferring an entitlement to registration as a British citizen on those British Overseas citizens, British subjects and British protected persons who have no other nationality and who have not, since 4 July 2002, given up any other nationality.

66.   Subsection (2) provides that any person registered under the new provision will be a British citizen "by descent" for the purposes of the 1981 Act.

Section 13:   British citizenship: registration of certain persons born between 1961 and 1983
67.   Section 13 inserts a new provision into the BNA 1981, conferring an entitlement to registration as a British citizen on persons born between 7 February 1961 and 1 January 1983 who, but for the inability (at that time) of women to pass on their citizenship, would have acquired British citizenship automatically when the BNA 1981 came into force on the latter of those two dates.

68.   Subsection (2) provides that any person registered under the new provision will be a British citizen "by descent" for the purposes of the 1981 Act.

Section 14: Hong Kong
69.   Section 14 re-enacts the substance of section 42(6) of the BNA 1981, by preventing registration as a British overseas territories citizen on the basis of a connection with Hong Kong.

Section 15: Repeal of spent provisions
70.   Section 15 introduces Schedule 2, which repeals certain sections of the BNA 1981 which are now spent. Paragraph 2 of Schedule 2 provides that the status of people who were registered under any of these sections is unaffected by the repeals.

PART 2: ACCOMMODATION CENTRES

Establishment
Section 16: Establishment of centres

71. This section enables the Secretary of State to arrange for the provision of premises to be used as accommodation centres. Subsection (3) enables the Secretary of State to arrange for the provision of facilities for the hearing of appeals at or near an accommodation centre and for facilities to be provided at an accommodation centre in connection with casework to determine asylum claims.

Use of centres
Section 17: Support for destitute asylum-seeker

72. Subsection (1) of section 17 gives the Secretary of State power to provide accommodation in an accommodation centre, or to arrange for the provision of such accommodation through another party (for example a local authority or private sector contractor). Accommodation in an accommodation centre may be provided to asylum-seekers and their dependants who are destitute or likely to become destitute within a period to be prescribed by regulations - this will allow the Secretary of State to start making arrangements in anticipation of actual destitution. "Asylum-seeker" is defined in section 18, "dependant" in section 20 and "destitution" in section 19. Subsection (2) enables the Secretary of State to make regulations about the procedure to be followed in providing accommodation in an accommodation centre and subsection (3) gives examples of the particular provisions which may be included in the regulations.

Section 18: Asylum-seeker: definition

73. Section 18 defines the term "asylum-seeker" as someone who is at least 18 years old, is in the UK and who has made a claim under the Refugee Convention or under article 3 ECHR, at a place designated by the Secretary of State, which has been recorded by the Secretary of State but which has not yet been determined. Once a person is no longer an asylum-seeker he will no longer be eligible for accommodation in an accommodation centre and will be expected to leave the accommodation centre, the period of time to be prescribed under section 21 (3) allowing him to make arrangements to do so. However, a person whose household includes a dependant child under the age of 18 will continue to be treated as an asylum-seeker whilst he and the child remain in the United Kingdom and will continue to be eligible for accommodation in an accommodation centre.

Section 19: Destitution: definition

74. Section 19 defines "destitution". This means a person, and his dependants if he has any, who is unable to obtain both adequate accommodation and food and other essential items. In deciding whether accommodation is adequate, the Secretary of

State must have regard to any prescribed matter but may not have regard to whether a person has an enforceable right to occupy accommodation, whether a person shares all or part of the accommodation, the location of the accommodation, whether it is temporary or permanent or any other prescribed matter.

75.   Subsection (5) enables the Secretary of State to make regulations specifying items which are or are not to be considered as essential items.

76.   Subsection (6) allows the Secretary of State to make regulations specifying when a person is not to be treated as destitute, enabling the Secretary of State to have regard to any income which a person or his dependant might reasonably be expected to have, or support or particular assets which are or might be available and to make provision for the valuation of these assets.

Section 20: Dependant: definition
77.   Section 20 defines a dependant of an asylum-seeker as someone who is in the United Kingdom and falls within a prescribed class.

Section 21: Sections 17 to 20: supplementary
78.   This section makes supplementary provision including provision that a claim for asylum is treated as determined after a prescribed period of time beginning with when the Secretary of State notifies the person of his decision on the claim or, if the person appeals against the decision, when the appeal is disposed of.   This section also gives the Secretary of State power to inquire into and decide a person's age for the purposes of assessing whether they are eligible for support.

Section 22: Immigration and Asylum Act 1999, s. 95
79.   Part VI of the 1999 Act sets out provisions for the support of asylum-seekers. Section 95 of that Act gives the Secretary of State the power to support destitute asylum-seekers and their dependants (if any) and section 96 sets out the ways in which support may be provided. Section 22 provides that the Secretary of State may provide support under section 95 of the 1999 Act by arranging for accommodation to be provided in an accommodation centre.

Section 23: Person subject to United Kingdom entrance control
80.   Paragraph 21(2) of Schedule 2 to the Immigration Act 1971 ("1971 Act") gives immigration officers the power to impose residence restrictions on people who are liable to detention under Schedule 2 to that Act. Paragraph 2(5) of Schedule 3 to the 1971 Act gives the Secretary of State the power to impose residence restrictions on people released from detention pending deportation. Subsections (1) and (2) of section 23 provide that these powers may be used to set a condition that a person must reside at an accommodation centre.

81.   Subsection (4) provides that a person who is required to leave an accommodation centre by virtue of section 26 (withdrawal of support) or for breach of residence conditions under section 30, will also have breached the condition imposed under

paragraph 21 (2) of Schedule 2 to the 1971 Act or paragraph 2(5) of Schedule 2 to that Act.

82.   Section 4 of the 1999 Act gives the Secretary of State a power to provide facilities for the accommodation of certain people, including those granted temporary admission to the United Kingdom or released from detention on bail. Subsection (5) of section 23 provides that the Secretary of State may provide support under section 4 of the 1999 Act by arranging for accommodation in an accommodation centre.

Section 24 : Provisional assistance

83.   Section 24 allows a person to be supported in an accommodation centre or provided with other support or assistance of any kind if the Secretary of State thinks that person might be eligible to be provided with accommodation in an accommodation centre pending a decision as to whether the person is in fact eligible for accommodation in an accommodation centre. Subsection (2) enables local authorities to provide support under this section in accordance with arrangements made by the Secretary of State.

Section 25: Length of stay

84.   Subsection (1) is subject to the provisions of subsection (2). Subsection (1) prevents the Secretary of State from requiring a person to reside in an accommodation centre if he has been a resident of an accommodation centre for a continuous period of six months. Subsection (2) enables the Secretary of State to require a person to remain in an accommodation centre for a maximum of 9 months if he thinks it appropriate in the particular circumstances of the case. Subsection (2) also makes clear that a person may choose to remain in an accommodation centre beyond the maximum periods contained in this section in agreement with the Secretary of State. Subsection (4) enables the Secretary of State to make an order to shorten the maximum periods.

Section 26: Withdrawal of support

85.   Section 26(1) sets out particular circumstances in which the Secretary of State may stop providing support to a person in an accommodation centre under section 17 or for whom provisional assistance under section 24 is being provided, namely: where the Secretary of State suspects a person or a dependant of his has committed an offence under the relevant provisions listed in section 35; and where the person or a dependant of his has failed to comply with the Secretary of State's directions as to the time and manner of travel to the accommodation centre or to other accommodation being provided under sections 17 or 24.

86.   Subsection (2) enables regulations to be made specifying other circumstances in which support under sections 17 and 24 may be stopped. Subsection (3) allows the Secretary of State to take into account the fact he has withdrawn support under this section or section 30 (breach of conditions of residence), or that circumstances exist in which he would have withdrawn support, in deciding whether to provide support under sections 17 (support for destitute asylum seekers) or 24 (provisional assistance) of the Act or under sections 4 (accommodation for those temporarily released from detention), 95 (persons for whom support may be provided) or 98 (temporary support) of the 1999 Act. Subsection (4) makes clear that section 26 does not affect the

right of appeal against refusal or withdrawal of support that is provided for in section 103 of the 1999 Act (as amended by Section 53).

Operation of centres
Section 27: Resident of centre

87.   Section 27 defines a resident of an accommodation centre for the purposes of Part 2.

Section 28: Manager of centre

88.   Section 28 defines a manager of an accommodation centre for the purposes of Part 2.

Section 29: Facilities

89.   Section 29 gives the Secretary of State the power to provide residents of accommodation centres with a number of facilities and services, described in subsection (1).

90.   Subsection (2) enables the Secretary of State by regulations to set the maximum amount of money that can be provided to the resident of an accommodation centre.

91.   Subsection (3) enables the Secretary of State to arrange for the provision of facilities in an accommodation centre for the use of legal advisers and subsection (4) requires the Secretary of State to take reasonable steps to ensure that a resident has an opportunity to obtain legal advice before the appointment made for his substantive asylum interview.

92.   Subsection (5) allows the Secretary of State to add by order to the list of items and facilities which may be provided to a resident of an accommodation centre set out in subsection (1). Orders and regulations under this section are subject to the negative resolution procedure under section 39.

Section 30: Conditions of residence

93.   Section 30 enables the Secretary of State to make regulations setting out conditions of residence that may be imposed on residents of accommodation centres. The powers to impose residence restrictions set out in paragraph 21 of Schedule 2 to the 1971 Act and paragraph 2 (5) of Schedule 3 to that Act are unaffected by this section.

94.   Subsection (3) sets out two particular conditions that may be imposed; subsection (4) makes clear that a resident who breaches a condition may be required to leave the centre, with his dependants (if any); subsection (5) provides that a resident and his dependants may be required to leave the centre if a dependant breaches a condition; and subsection (6) provides that the regulations setting the conditions under this section must include a provision for making sure that residents are informed in writing of any condition imposed on them. Regulations under section 30 are subject to the affirmative resolution procedure under section 39.

Section 31: Financial contribution by resident

95.   Section 31 provides that conditions imposed under section 30 may require a resident of an accommodation centre to make payments to the Secretary of State or the

manager of the centre where the resident applied to be supported and had assets (including assets outside the United Kingdom) at the time of the application which at that time were not capable of being realised but have since become realisable.

96.   Subsection (4) provides the methods by which any amounts may be recovered.

Section 32: Tenure

97.   Section 32 provides that a resident of an accommodation centre is not to be treated as acquiring a tenancy of or other interest in any part of the centre. It allows the Secretary of State, or the manager of the centre if authorised to do so by the Secretary of State, to recover possession of the premises occupied by the resident where the resident is required to leave the centre or where the Secretary of State decides to stop providing accommodation in the centre for that resident.

98.   Subsection (4) makes clear that any licence to occupy premises which a resident of an accommodation centre has will be an excluded licence for the purposes of the Protection from Eviction Act 1977. There is therefore no need to obtain a court order before recovering possession of the premises. The procedure to be followed in order to recover the premises is to be prescribed in regulations. Subsection (7) means that accommodation provided under Section 24 (1) (b) (i.e. provisional accommodation not in an accommodation centre) is to be treated as an accommodation centre for the purposes of Section 32.

Section 33: Advisory Groups

99.   Section 33 requires the Secretary of State to appoint an Advisory Group for each accommodation centre. Subsection (2) enables the Secretary of State to make regulations conferring functions on Advisory Groups and making provision about the constitution and proceedings of the Advisory Groups. Subsection (3) requires the regulations to provide for members of Advisory Groups to visit the accommodation centre, to hear complaints made by residents of the centre and to report to the Secretary of State. Subsection (4) requires the manager of an accommodation centre to permit a member of the Advisory Group to visit the centre at any time and to visit any resident of the centre at any time, provided the resident consents. Subsection (5) makes provision about the terms of appointments for members of the Advisory Groups and subsection (6) enables the Secretary of State to pay expenses of members and to make facilities available to them.

General

Section 34: The Monitor of Accommodation Centres

100.   Section 34 requires the Secretary of State to appoint a Monitor of Accommodation Centres. The Monitor may not be a person who is employed within a government department. Subsection (2) requires the Monitor to monitor the operation of Part 2 of the Act and, in particular, to consider the quality and effectiveness of accommodation and other facilities provided, the nature and enforcement of conditions of residence, the treatment of residents, and whether the location of an accommodation centre prevents a need of its residents from being met. Subsection (3) requires the Monitor

to consult the Secretary of State and such other persons as he considers appropriate. Subsections (4) and (5) require the Monitor to make an annual report to the Secretary of State, which will be laid before Parliament, and to report on such other occasions as the Secretary of State may request. Subsections (6), (7) and (8) make provision relating to the terms of appointment, the payment of fees and expenses and a power for the Secretary of State to appoint more than one person to act jointly as Monitor.

Section 35: Ancillary provisions

101. This Section provides that specified provisions of the 1999 Act shall apply for the purposes of Part 2 of the Act as they do for Part VI of that Act. In particular, subsections (1)(a) to (d) of this section provide that certain criminal offences that apply to the provision of support for asylum-seekers under Part VI of the 1999 Act, shall also apply for the purposes of this Part.

102. Subsections (1)(f) and (1)(g) apply provisions in Part VI of the 1999 Act relating to recovery by the Secretary of State of monies provided to support asylum-seekers as a result of fraud or material non-disclosure of facts or where a sponsor has failed to maintain a person he undertook to maintain.

103. Section 124 of the 1999 Act, applied to Part 2 of the Act by subsection (1)(h), makes provision for the Secretary of State to be a corporation sole for the purpose of holding property . This will assist in conveyancing if the Secretary of State acquires property for the purposes of Part 2. Section 127 of the 1999 Act, applied to Part 2 of the Act by subsection (1)(i) relates to powers for the Secretary of State to require certain information from property owners about premises in which accommodation has been provided for the purposes of support.

Section 36: Education: general

104. Section 36(1) provides that residents of an accommodation centre shall not be treated as part of the population of a local education authority ("LEA") for the purposes of section 13 of the Education Act 1996 ("the EA 1996"). Section 13 of the EA 1996 describes, in general terms, the duties of a LEA towards the population of its area. The LEA has a duty to contribute towards the spiritual, moral, mental and physical development of the community by securing that efficient primary and secondary education is available to meet the needs of the population of their area .

105. Section 36(2) prohibits a child who is a resident of an accommodation centre from attending a maintained school or nursery.

106. The prohibition on a child who is a resident of an accommodation centre attending a maintained school or nursery under subsection (2) is qualified by section 36(3) which enables such a child to attend a community special school or a foundation special school if it is named in a statement of special educational needs in respect of the child made under section 324 of the Education Act 1996.

107. For residents of accommodation centres, section 36(5)(a) removes the duties in

section 86 of the School Standards and Framework Act 1998 Act requiring LEAs to enable the parents of children in their area to express a preference as to the school at which they want their children to be educated and to comply with any preference expressed.

108.   For residents of accommodation centres, section 36(5)(e) removes the duties in paragraph 3 of Schedule 27 to the EA 1996 requiring LEAs to enable the parents of children with special educational needs to express a preference as to the school at which they want their children to be educated, and the duty to specify the name of such a school in a child's statement of special educational needs.

109.   Section 36(6) provides that the power of the Special Educational Needs Tribunal under section 326(3) of the EA 1996 to order an LEA to amend a child's statement of special educational needs is subject to qualified prohibition on a child who is a resident of an accommodation centre attending a maintained school or nursery under section 36(2).

110.   Section 36(7) provides that a child who is resident in an accommodation centre and who has special educational needs shall be educated in the accommodation centre unless it is incompatible with (a) his receiving the special educational provision which his learning difficulty calls for, (b) the provision of efficient education for other children who are residents of the centre, or (c) the efficient use of resources.

111.   Section 36(8) provides that a person exercising functions under the Act cannot rely on section 36(7)(b) and claim that it is not compatible with the provision of efficient education for other children who are residents of the accommodation centre for a child with special educational needs to be educated in the centre, unless there is no action that could reasonably be taken by that person or by any other person who exercises functions in respect of the centre to make section 36{7}(b) not apply.

112.   Section 36(10) provides that subsections (1), (2) and (5) above shall not apply in relation to an accommodation centre if education is not provided for children who are residents of the centre under section 29(1)(f).

Section 37: Education: special cases
113.   This Section makes provision for a LEA to provide education for a child resident in an accommodation centre in certain circumstances.

114.   Section 37(1) provides that this section applies if a person who provides education to residents of accommodation centres recommends in writing to the local education authority for the area in which the centre is located that this section should apply to a particular child.

115.   Section 37(2) provides that a LEA may arrange for the provision of education for a child to whom this section applies and disapply a provision of section 36 in respect of

that child.

116.	Section 37(4) requires the governing body of a maintained school to comply with a requirement of the LEA to admit a child to whom this section applies to the school. The duty imposed on the governing body of a maintained school is qualified by section 37(5) which provides that subsection (4) shall not apply where compliance with such a requirement would prejudice measures taken for the purpose of complying with a duty to comply with the limit on infant class sizes.

117.	Section 37(6) requires the LEA to consult in accordance with regulations before imposing a requirement under subsection (4) for a school's governing body to admit a pupil.

Section 38: Local authority

118.	Section 38 enables local authorities in accordance with arrangements made by the Secretary of State, to arrange for the provision of an accommodation centre, to make premises available for an accommodation centre and to provide services in connection with an accommodation centre. Subsection (2) sets out a number of functions that a local authority may do under this section, including the provision of services outside its area and tendering for or entering into a contract.

Section 39: "Prescribed": orders and regulations

119.	Section 39 sets out the procedure to be used when making an order or regulations under this Part of the Act.

Section 40: Scotland

120.	This section provides that the Secretary of State may not make arrangements for establishing an accommodation centre in Scotland unless he has consulted the Scottish Ministers. It also provides for the Secretary of State to make provision by order, subject to the negative resolution procedure, for the education of residents of accommodation centres in Scotland.

Section 41: Northern Ireland

121.	Section 41 makes equivalent provision to section 40 for Northern Ireland.

Section 42: Wales

122.	Section 42 requires the Secretary of State to consult the National Assembly for Wales before making arrangements for an accommodation centre in Wales.

PART 3: OTHER SUPPORT AND ASSISTANCE

Section 43: Asylum-seeker: form of support

123.	Section 43 creates an order-making power under which support provided for asylum-seekers under section 96(1)(b) of the 1999 Act can be restricted to those asylum-seekers who have accommodation provided for them under section 96(1)(a) of the

1999 Act. An Order made under this power can apply generally or in specific circumstances. Any Order made under this provision must be approved in draft by both Houses of Parliament before it can be made.

Section 44: Destitute asylum-seeker

124. Section 44 amends various provisions of Part VI of the 1999 Act (support for asylum seekers), to bring them into line with the provisions of Part 2 of the Act. Subsections (1) to (5) amend parts of section 94 of the 1999 Act to bring the definitions in relation to the meaning of "asylum seeker" and "dependant" in that section into line with those used in sections 18 and 20 of this Act. Subsection (6) substitutes a new provision for section 95(2) to (8) of the 1999 Act, which defines destitution for the purposes of support under that section. It mirrors section 19 (in relation to accommodation centres) by defining a person as destitute when that person does not have, and cannot obtain, both adequate accommodation and food and other essential items. This replaces the original provision in section 95 (2) but the effect is the same. Subsection (6) also mirrors section 19 by providing the factors to which the Secretary of State cannot have regard in determining when accommodation is adequate and what items are essential items. Like section 19, the Secretary of State also has the power to provide for when a person is not to be treated as destitute.

Section 45: Section 44: supplemental

125. Subsections (1) to (3) of section 45 make consequential amendments to the 1999 Act to reflect the changes made to section 95 of that Act by section 44. Subsections (5) to (7) make consequential amendments to certain social welfare provisions, that were amended by the 1999 Act, to take account of the changes which section 44 makes to section 95(2) to 95(8) of that Act.

Section 46: Section 44: supplemental: Scotland and Northern Ireland

126. This section makes further consequential amendments to social welfare provisions in relation to Scotland and Northern Ireland. These social welfare provisions were amended by the 1999 Act and now need to be amended to reflect the changes made to section 95(2) to (8) of the 1999 Act by section 44 of this Act.

Section 47: Asylum-seeker: family with children

127. Section 47 extends section 122 of the 1999 Act to accommodation centres by inserting a new section 122 into the 1999 Act. The new section 122 places a duty on the Secretary of State, where support under section 95 of the 1999 Act or section 17 of this Act is applied for by a person whom the Secretary of State thinks is eligible for support, to offer support under one of those provisions where the asylum seeker's household includes a dependant child under the age of 18. It also prevents local authorities from assisting a child under various provisions of the Children Act 1989 (or equivalent Scottish or Northern Irish legislation) if the Secretary of State has offered support in respect of the child and that offer remains open, or if the Secretary of State is providing the child with support under section 95 of the 1999 Act or section 17 of this Act, or has indicated that he would offer to support the child if an application for support were made, subject to any order disapplying subsection (3) made under subsection (5). Where support has been offered or provided

21

pursuant to this section but later withdrawn, subsection (6) provides that only the local authority within whose area the withdrawn support was provided may provide assistance under the various child welfare provisions set out in subsection (4).

Section 48: Young asylum-seeker

128. Section 48(a) provides a power for the Secretary of State to make payments to local authorities under section 110 of the 1999 Act to reimburse them for the support they have provided for Unaccompanied Asylum-Seeking Children (UASCs). The Secretary of State already makes these payments but requires a special grant report under the Local Government Finance Act 1988. The definition of asylum-seeker in section 94(1) of the 1999 Act excludes those who are under the age of 18 and, therefore, payments under section 110 of the 1999 Act cannot currently be made in respect of those who are under the age of 18. Section 48 will enable payments under section 110 to be made in respect of asylum-seekers that are under the age of 18. The new power does not affect the amounts to be paid to local authorities or the requirements for auditing claims and ensuring payments only relate to those entitled. Section 48(b) provides a similar power for the Secretary of State to make payments to voluntary organisations under section 111 of the 1999 Act in respect of UASCs.

Section 49: Failed asylum-seeker

129. Section 49 gives the Secretary of State additional powers to support failed asylum-seekers. Section 4 of the 1999 Act currently provides that the Secretary of State may provide, or arrange for the provision of, accommodation of persons temporarily admitted to the United Kingdom or released from detention as specified in paragraphs (a), (b) and (c) of that section. However, the existing power does not allow the provision of accommodation to all categories of asylum-seekers whose claims for asylum have been rejected, should the Secretary of State decide to provide such accommodation in particular cases. Section 49 remedies this.

Section 50: Conditions of support

130. Section 95(9) of the 1999 Act provides that support for asylum-seekers (accommodation and subsistence) may be provided subject to conditions. Section 50 provides a power for the Secretary of State to link the provision of support (accommodation and subsistence) with compliance with the conditions on which temporary admission or release from detention has been granted.

Section 51: Choice of form of support

131. Section 51 provides that the Secretary of State may refuse support under sections 17 or 24 of this Act, or under section 4, section 95 or section 98 of the 1999 Act to a person if that person has already been offered support under one of those provisions. The Secretary of State is given a discretion as to the provision under which he may choose to offer support.

Section 52: Back-dating of benefit for refugee

132. Section 123(7) of the 1999 Act provides that where a person who has been recognised as a refugee within the meaning of the Refugee Convention, or a dependant of such a

person, makes a claim for any benefit to which he would have been entitled had he been regarded as a refugee when he made his claim for asylum and has received support under Part VI of the 1999 Act, regulations may make provision for the value of that support to be offset against the backdated payment of any benefit. Section 52 extends the provisions of section 123(7) of the 1999 Act to persons provided with support under Part 2 of the Act.

Section 53: Asylum-seeker: appeal against refusal to support

133. Section 53 makes provision for appeals against refusal of asylum support or the ending of support. This section substitutes sections 103, 103A and 103B for the existing section 103 of the 1999 Act.

134. The provisions substituted for the existing section 103 of the 1999 Act extend the existing rights of appeal against refusal or ending of support under section 95 of the 1999 Act to refusal or ending of support under section 17 of the Act which provides for support in accommodation centres (new section 103(1)-(3)). This section also re-enacts provisions of the 1999 Act relating to appeals to the asylum support adjudicators and extends them to support under section 17 (new section 103(4)-(5)). It also re-enacts the provision of the 1999 Act providing for the payment of reasonable travelling expenses incurred by an appellant in connection with attending an appeal hearing under section 103 or 103A and extends this to section 17 (new section 103B).

Section 54 and Schedule 3: Withholding and withdrawal of support

135. This section introduces Schedule 3, which restricts the type of support and accommodation that is provided to those who are European Union (EU)/European Economic Area (EEA) citizens; those with refugee status in other EU/EEA states; failed asylum seekers and persons unlawfully present in the UK.

136. Paragraph 1 (1) (a) – (m) of Schedule 3 lists the various pieces of legislation in England and Wales, Scotland and Northern Ireland under which support and/or accommodation to individuals in these categories will be restricted.

137. Sub-paragraph (2) provides that any powers or duties imposed by the legislation in Paragraph 1 may not be exercised in respect of any person to whom this applies, regardless of whether that person has received support or not in the past.

138. Paragraph 2 provides a safety net to children under 18. Children will remain eligible for support or assistance, as will adults provided for in regulations as eligible to receive it. Further, this paragraph allows the Secretary of State, by regulation, to extend the categories of those persons eligible for support.

139. Paragraph 3 addresses our international obligations. Nothing prevents local authorities or the National Asylum Support Service (NASS) exercising powers or performing duties to the extent that it is necessary to avoid breaching any European Convention on Human Rights (ECHR) right or a person's rights under the European Community treaties.

140.   Paragraph 4 details the first class of people ineligible for support. If an individual has refugee status in another EEA Member State, or is the dependant of a person who is in the UK and has refugee status in another EEA Member State, they are ineligible for support.

141.   Paragraph 5 makes citizens of other EEA member states ineligible for support if they are not present in the UK exercising Community Treaty rights or they are residing in the UK but Community Treaties forbid the person being supported from public funds.

142.   Paragraph 6 makes failed asylum seekers ineligible for further support if they have failed to co-operate with removal directions issued in respect of them.

143.   Paragraph 7 provides that persons who are unlawfully present in the UK, and who are not asylum-seekers, are ineligible for support.

144.   Paragraph 8 allows the Secretary of State to make arrangements, by regulation, for citizens of other EU/EEA states and those with refugee status in other EU/EEA states to be provided with a journey home.

145.   Paragraph 9 allows the Secretary of State to make arrangements, by regulation, for persons to be provided with accommodation until the time of their journey home. Only persons with dependent children will have accommodation arranged. Paragraph 10 makes the same arrangement for persons unlawfully in the UK. Again, only persons with dependent children will be provided with accommodation **as long as they have not failed to** co-operate with removal directions issued in respect of them.

146.   Paragraph 11 provides further powers in relation to the regulation- making power.

147.   Paragraph 12 enables provision to be made in regulation in respect of persons who refuse the offer of a journey home or fail to travel or co-operate with efforts being made to enable them to leave the UK. It allows regulations to be made that ensure only new arrangements enabling a person to leave can be made, but no additional accommodation can be provided. Sub-paragraph (2) allows for regulations to make exception for people who are unable to travel for a defined acceptable reason, and who can provide the required proof of the reason.

148.   Sub-paragraph (1) of paragraph 13 creates a new criminal offence. It will be an offence for a person to accept temporary accommodation and/or travel assistance to another country then return to the UK and make another request for an arrangement to be made under paragraph 8, 9, or 10, i.e. travel assistance or temporary accommodation. Sub paragraph (2) creates an additional criminal offence. It will be an offence for a person who has previously requested arrangements be made for him to fail to mention this in any future application. Both offences are punishable on conviction by imprisonment for a term not exceeding six months.

149.   Paragraph 14 places an obligation upon local authorities to inform the Secretary of

State of any person they suspect or know to be unlawfully present in the UK or a failed asylum seeker.

150.   Paragraph 15 allows the Secretary of State to amend the Schedule by order so as to remove or add categories of persons ineligible for support, to add or remove other statutes to the list of those which might provide support or assistance, and to add, amend or remove any limitations or exceptions to the list.

Section 55: Late claim for asylum: refusal of support
151.   Section 55 makes provision to restrict access to support provided to asylum seekers under certain provisions of the 1999 Act and this Act and under certain provisions of housing and local government legislation in cases where the Secretary of State is not satisfied that a person has made his asylum application as soon as reasonably practicable after his arrival in the United Kingdom. Section 55 is intended to put the burden of proof on the asylum seeker claiming support to satisfy the Secretary of State that he made his asylum claim as soon as reasonably practicable after he arrived in the UK. If he cannot so satisfy the Secretary of State then the provision of support is prohibited.

152.   Subsection (1) provides that the Secretary of State may not provide or arrange for the provision of support to a person under a provision mentioned in subsection (2) of the section to a person who has claimed asylum if the Secretary of State is not satisfied that the person has made his claim for asylum as soon as reasonably practicable after his arrival in the United Kingdom.

153.   Subsection (2) specifies the provisions of the 1999 Act and of this Act under which support may not be provided in the circumstances specified in subsection (1) of the section.

154.   Subsection (3) provides that a local authority may not provide or arrange for the provision of support to a person under a provision mentioned in subsection (4) of the section to a person who has claimed asylum whom Secretary of State is not satisfied has made his asylum application as soon as reasonably practicable after his arrival in the United Kingdom.

155.   Subsection (4) specifies the provisions of certain housing and local government legislation under which support may not be provided in the circumstances specified in subsection (3) of the section.

156.   Subsection (5) provides that section 55 shall not prevent the Secretary of State exercising his power to provide support to the extent necessary to avoid the breach of a person's rights under ECHR or to children and their families under section 95 of the 1999 Act, section 17 of this Act, section 98 of the 1999 Act or section 24 of this Act.

157.   Subsection (6)(a) and (b) stipulate that a local authority that proposes to provide or arrange for the provision of support under a provision mentioned in subsection (4) of this section must inform the Secretary of State if the authority believes the person

has made a claim for asylum and must act in accordance with any guidance issued by the Secretary of State to determine whether subsection (3) of this section (the provision preventing support in certain circumstances) applies.

158.   Subsection (6)(c) provides that a local authority shall not be prevented from providing support where it has complied with the requirements of the previous two paragraphs of this subsection and has concluded that the prohibition on providing support does not apply.

159.   Subsection (7) enables the Secretary of State by order to amend the list of provisions specified in subsection (4) of this section.

160.   Subsection (8) specifies the procedure for making an order under subsection (7) and makes provision for it to include transitional, consequential or incidental provision.

161.   Subsection (9) provides that "claim for asylum" has the same meaning as in section 18 of this Act, thereby removing any uncertainty as to how it is to be interpreted.

162.   Subsection (10) provides that a decision by the Secretary of State that the section prevents him from providing or arranging for the provision of support under this section does not attract a right of appeal to the Asylum Support Adjudicators under section 103 of the 1999 Act.

163.   Subsection (11) provides that the section does not prevent a person residing in a place in accordance with a residence restriction imposed in reliance on section 70 of this Act.

Section 56: Provision of support by local authority

164.   Section 56 makes provision to enable local authorities to provide support under section 98 of the 1999 Act to asylum seekers pending the determination by the Secretary of State of a claim for support under section 95 of the 1999 Act. This support may be provided in any of the ways mentioned in sections 96(1) and 96(2) of the 1999 Act.

Section 57: Application for support: false or incomplete information

165.   Section 57 makes additional provision in respect of regulations about asylum support made under paragraph 12 of Schedule 8 to the 1999 Act. The section provides that such regulations may provide for an application for asylum support not to be entertained where the Secretary of State is not satisfied that information provided by an applicant is complete or accurate or that the applicant is co-operating with enquiries under paragraph 12 (d) of Schedule 8 to the 1999 Act.

Section 58: Voluntary departure from United Kingdom

166.   Section 58 allows the Secretary of State to make arrangements to assist "voluntary leavers". A person qualifies for assistance as a "voluntary leaver" if he is leaving the United Kingdom for a place where he hopes to take up permanent residence and if the Secretary of State thinks it is in his interests to leave the United Kingdom and

that he wishes to do so. British citizens and EEA nationals are excluded.

167. Section 58 replaces section 29 of the 1971 Act. The class of person who qualifies for assistance has been largely unchanged (the only difference is that section 58 now excludes EEA nationals as well as British citizens), but the sort of assistance which can be given has been expanded. In addition to meeting travel expenses of voluntary leavers and their families, the Secretary of State is now able to meet costs associated with their immediate arrival and reception and longer-term support to facilitate successful re-integration. It is also able to fund "explore and prepare" visits by persons who wish to assess the possibility of becoming voluntary leavers.

168. The Home Office is currently responsible for a number of schemes to assist "voluntary return". The existing schemes are being run for the Home Office by the International Organisation for Migration in partnership with Refugee Action. Section 58 enables the Secretary of State to make payments directly to these organisations.

Section 59: International projects

169. Section 59 provides a power for the Secretary of State to participate in certain projects, either with other Governments, the EU or other non-governmental organisations of a domestic or international nature. The types of projects in respect of which this power to participate may be exercised are set out in subsection (1). Such projects may have as their aim, amongst others, the return of migrants both inside and outside of the United Kingdom to their country of origin by voluntary or compulsory means. For example participation in projects for the resettlement of refugees run by the UN would fall within this provision. Subsection (2) clarifies that the power to participate may be exercised by the Secretary of State in a way that involves the provision of funding to both governmental and non-governmental organisations, both in the United Kingdom and abroad.

170. Pilot projects of the type authorised by this provision have already been undertaken, funded by the Secretary of State under the terms of the Appropriation Act. The terms of this Act are not sufficient to enable the funding of projects on a long-term basis.

171. Subsection (4) makes clear that no new power of removal is created by this section, nor are the rights to enter or remain of individuals affected in any way by it.

Section 60: Northern Ireland Authorities

172. Section 60 amends the definition of a Northern Ireland authority in the 1999 Act to ensure it is wide enough for the purposes of emergency accommodation, induction and accommodation centres.

Section 61: Repeal of spent provisions

173. This section repeals sections 96(4) to (6) and section 166(4)(e) of the Immigration and Asylum Act 1999.

PART 4: DETENTION AND REMOVAL

Detention
Section 62: Detention by Secretary of State

174. Under paragraph 16 of Schedule 2 to the 1971 Act, an immigration officer has the power to detain an arriving passenger, an illegal entrant or a passenger liable to removal under the powers contained in section 10 of the 1999 Act. As an alternative to detaining them, the immigration officer also has the power (under paragraph 21 of Schedule 2 to the 1971 Act) to temporarily admit them to the United Kingdom. The Secretary of State has the power (under Schedule 3 to the 1971 Act) to detain or release someone against whom deportation action is being taken. The Secretary of State also has the power to grant temporary admission to someone who has made a claim for asylum immediately on arrival at a port, but unlike an immigration officer, has no power to detain such a person.

175. This section will give the Secretary of State the same power to detain as immigration officers, in the following circumstances - (1) pending a decision by the Secretary of State whether to set removal directions under paragraph 10, 10A or 14 of Schedule 2 to the 1971 Act and pending removal; and (2) where the Secretary of State has power to examine a person or grant or refuse them leave to enter under section 3A of the 1971 Act, pending the examination, his decision to give or refuse leave to enter, his decision to set removal directions or removal of such a person.

176. Subsections (3)(a) and (3)(c) are intended to ensure that a person detained under this section has the same rights as persons detained under Schedule 2 to the 1971 Act to apply for bail. Subsection (3)(b) allows the Secretary of State, where he has power to detain under this section, as an alternative, to grant temporary admission or release from detention under paragraph 21 of Schedule 2 to the 1971 Act in the same way that an immigration officer currently can.

177. This will mean that the decision whether or not to detain can be taken by the person who determines a person's asylum claim or immigration status and that this can be done at the same time.

178. Subsection (4) allows restrictions under paragraph 21 of Schedule 2 to the 1971 Act set by the Secretary of State to be varied by an immigration officer and vice versa. The present offence of failing to comply with a condition of temporary admission or release without reasonable excuse is extended by subsection (9) to include failing to comply with a condition set by the Secretary of State.

179. Subsections (10) to (16) are consequential amendments to ensure that relevant provisions in other legislation to persons detained under the 1971 Act include references to persons detained under this section.

Section 63: Control of entry to United Kingdom, &c: use of force

180. This section ensures consistency of language between the powers of escorts and immigration officers to use force. It makes no substantive change to the powers of the latter.

Section 64: Escorts

181. Section 54 amends paragraph 17 of Schedule 2 to the 1971 Act so as to confer a power on detainee custody officers, acting in accordance with escort arrangements, to enter premises in order to search a person who has been detained prior to escorting him to a place of detention. The power is confined to those circumstances where an immigration or police officer has executed a warrant issued under paragraph 17(2) of Schedule 2 to the 1971 Act and has detained a person on the premises.

182. The existing powers of detainee custody officers acting in accordance with escort arrangements are contained in paragraph 2 of Schedule 13 to the 1999 Act. In particular, a detainee custody officer has the power to search a detained person for whose delivery or custody he is responsible. The new power would permit such a search to take place on private premises where entry is not by consent.

Section 65: Detention centres: custodial functions

183. Section 65 amends section 154(5) of the 1999 Act so as to clarify the basis on which prison officers or prisoner custody officers may perform the functions of detainee custody officers in detention centres. The amendment will mean that the functions of detainee custody officers may be conferred on prison officers or prisoner custody officers without the Secretary of State having, as at present, to consider it <u>necessary</u> to do so. The section also makes consequential amendments to Schedules 11 and 12 to the 1999 Act, which relate to the powers and duties of detainee custody officers and to discipline within detention centres, so as to apply the provisions of these Schedules to prison officers or prisoner custody officers performing the functions of detainee custody officers in detention centres.

Section 66: Detention centres: change of name

184. Section 66 amends section 147 of the 1999 Act so that detention centres will be known formally as removal centres. This reflects the part played by detention in the removal of failed asylum-seekers and others. There are a number of minor and consequential amendments to other provisions in the 1999 Act and provisions in other legislation that refer to "detention centres". There are no substantive changes to the existing provisions relating to the purpose and operation of detention centres.

Section 67: Construction of reference to a person liable to detention

185. A person who is liable to be detained, or who is actually detained, under the powers contained in the Immigration Acts, may instead be granted temporary admission or temporary release. This status may be subject to restrictions such as requiring the person concerned to live at a particular address and/or to report to the police or an immigration officer.

186.   The powers to detain in immigration legislation do not specify a maximum period beyond which a person cannot be detained. However, for the detention to be lawful, it has to be for the purpose stated, and the person may only be detained for a period that is reasonable in all the circumstances of the particular case. Thus, for example, where a person is detained under paragraph 16(2) of Schedule 2 to the 1971 Act pending a decision whether or not to give directions for their removal or, where such directions have been given, pending their removal, they can only be detained for as long as the event can reasonably be described as "pending". Once that point has been passed, the detention is no longer lawful.

187.   Where this occurs, the practice has been to grant temporary release, generally subject to the conditions described above.

188.   A judgment by the High Court in July 2002 (in the case of *Hwez and Khadir*) held that this practice was unlawful.   The judge in that case held that the phrase "liable to detention" in paragraph 21 of Schedule 2 to the 1971 Act did not relate to the categories of person subject to immigration control who could, at some point, be detained, but rather was limited to those cases where the individual concerned could lawfully be detained at that precise moment. Thus, once the point was reached where the power to detain no longer existed, the alternative of temporary release subject to conditions was no longer available either.   Similar considerations would apply to deportation cases, where the power to detain or release subject to restrictions is contained in Schedule 3 to the 1971 Act, rather than Schedule 2.

189.   The purpose of this section is to avoid a situation where people subject to immigration control, who do not have leave to be here, but who cannot lawfully be detained, are left at large without there being any way of keeping track of them. The power to impose reporting and residence conditions on asylum seekers and others while their claims to remain in the United Kingdom are being considered is for contact management purposes, and this power is dependant on there being a power to grant temporary admission or release.

190.   As subsection (1)(a) makes clear, this section does not affect the scope of the current powers to detain. It only applies to provisions which do not actually confer a power to detain. What it does is define what a reference in immigration legislation to being "liable to detention" means, making it clear that the term includes cases where the only reason the person cannot be detained at that precise moment is one of those specified in subsection (2).

191.   The effect of this is that the people concerned can be given temporary admission or release (under Schedule 2 to the 1971 Act) or released on conditions (under Schedule 3) even where they may not lawfully be detained under the detention powers in, respectively, Schedule 2 and Schedule 3 to the 1971 Act.

192.   Subsection (3) gives the section retrospective effect, thus avoiding the need to reassess the cases of persons on temporary admission on an individual basis. Because the provision will always have applied, it has   the   effect   of   validating   the

authorisation of temporary admission and restrictions imposed.

Temporary release
Section 68: Bail

193. Section 68 provides a power for the Secretary of State, or an official acting on his behalf, to grant bail to a person detained under paragraph 16 of Schedule 2 to the 1971 Act in the same circumstances as a chief immigration officer may currently. The power takes effect after the expiry of the eighth day after detention begins, prior to which the power to grant bail will continue to be exercised by an immigration officer not below the rank of chief immigration officer.

194. Section 68 also repeals Part III of the 1999 Act, with the exceptions of sections 53 (except subsection (5)) and 54. Part III of the 1999 Act contained provisions for a system of routine bail hearings for those in detention and has not been implemented. The rights to apply for bail under existing legislation will remain in place.

Section 69: Reporting restriction: travel expenses

195. Section 50 provides a power for the Secretary of State to link the provision of support with a requirement to report to the police or an immigration officer. Section 69 enables the Secretary of State to meet the reasonable travel costs of supported asylum-seekers who are required to travel to enable them to report as directed.

Section 70: Induction

196. Section 70 provides that an asylum-seeker and any dependants may be required to reside at a location for a period of up to 14 days which is at or near a place where a programme of induction will take place. The intention is that all asylum-seekers will be given an induction at the outset of their claim. The purpose of this induction is to inform the asylum-seeker about how the asylum process will work, up to and beyond the initial decision on their claim; to explain what responsibilities they have to comply with requirements placed upon them as part of that process; and to consider any requests for support. The residence restriction can be imposed regardless of circumstances, for example, whether or not the asylum-seeker has alternative accommodation available to them.

Section 71: Asylum-seeker: residence, &c. restriction

197. Section 71 is concerned with asylum-seekers who have existing leave to enter or remain at the time they make a claim for asylum (at present, only a small percentage of asylum-seekers fall into this category). The section provides that such asylum-seekers and their dependants may have restrictions imposed on them which can be imposed on other asylum-seekers (that is, those without existing leave to enter or remain) under paragraph 21 of Schedule 2 to the 1971 Act. The powers under that paragraph include the power to impose reporting and residence requirements. The purpose of this provision is to ensure that all asylum-seekers, whatever their circumstances prior to making a claim, can be subject to the same basic process including, for example, the requirement to keep in touch through regular reporting. The section further provides that where an asylum-seeker with existing leave fails to

comply with a restriction placed upon him they will then become liable to detention under paragraph 16 of Schedule 2 to the 1971 Act. Restrictions imposed under this section cease to have effect once a person ceases to be an asylum-seeker.

Removal
Section 72: Serious criminal

198.   Article 33(1) of the Refugee Convention. prevents a refugee being returned to a place where their life or freedom is threatened. Article 33(1) does not apply where the refugee has been convicted of a particularly serious crime and is a danger to the community, by virtue of Article 33(2). The section provides that where a person is convicted in the United Kingdom of an offence and sentenced to a period of imprisonment of at least two years, or of an offence specified by order made by the Secretary of State, he will be presumed to have been convicted of a particularly serious crime and to be a danger to the community. Provision is made for convictions for offences outside the United Kingdom. A person may rebut the presumption that they have committed a particularly serious crime and are a danger to the community.

199.   Subsection (8) provides that the dangers a person may face if removed are not relevant to a consideration of whether the Article 33(2) presumption established by this section applies. Subsection (10) provides that where the Secretary of State has issued a certificate that the presumption applies an adjudicator, the Tribunal or the Special Immigration Appeals Commission must begin its substantive consideration of an appeal by looking at the certificate. If the appellate body agrees that the presumptions apply, having given opportunity for rebuttal, it must dismiss that part of the appeal which relates to removal being contrary to the Refugee Convention.

Section 73: Family

200.   Under paragraphs 8 to 10 of Schedule 2 to the 1971 Act, directions may be given for the removal of persons refused leave to enter the United Kingdom and illegal entrants. Subsection (1) allows removal directions to be given for the children of such people where those children were born in the United Kingdom.

201.   An equivalent power already exists under section 10(1)(c) of the 1999 Act in respect of children born in the United Kingdom whose parents have remained beyond their leave, breached the conditions of their leave or obtained leave to remain by deception.

202.   Subsections (2) to (4) make minor amendments in relation to the existing provisions of section 10 of the 1999 Act.

Section 74: Deception

203.   Under section 10(1)(b) of the 1999 Act, there is a power to remove immigration offenders who have obtained leave to remain by deception. Section 74 creates a power to remove people whose deception is discovered before leave is granted. (People who seek to obtain leave to remain by deception and people who succeed in doing so both commit an offence under section 24A(1)(a) of the 1971 Act.)

Section 75: Exemption from deportation

204.   Under section 7(1)(a) of the 1971 Act Commonwealth citizens or citizens of the Republic of Ireland cannot be deported on grounds of the public good if they: (a) were Commonwealth or Republic of Ireland citizens on 1st January 1973 (the date of the coming into force of the 1971 Act); (b) were ordinarily resident in the United Kingdom at that time; and (c) have been ordinarily resident in the United Kingdom ever since.

205.   Under section 7(1)(b) of 1971 Act Commonwealth citizens and citizens of the Republic of Ireland cannot be deported if they were ordinarily resident here on 1 January 1973 and have been ordinarily resident here for the 5 years prior to a decision to make a deportation order. Clearly, someone who has been ordinarily resident here at all times since 1 January 1973 has also been resident here for 5 years before the decision to deport. Subsection (2) therefore repeals section 7(1)(a) of the 1971 Act which is redundant.

206.   Subsection (3) replaces section 7(1)(b) of the 1971 Act.

Section 76: Revocation of leave to enter or remain
207.   Section 76 gives the Secretary of State power to revoke a person's indefinite leave to enter or remain in certain specified circumstances.

208.   Subsection (1) allows the Secretary of State to revoke indefinite leave where the person is liable to deportation but the person cannot be deported for legal reasons. An example of how this power might be used would be where a person has committed a serious criminal offence such that their deportation would be conducive to the public good but where they cannot be deported to their country of origin because removal would be contrary to Article 3 of the European Convention on Human Rights.

209.   Subsection (2) allows the Secretary of State to revoke the indefinite leave of persons who are liable to removal on the grounds that they obtained the leave by deception, but who cannot be removed for legal or practical reasons. Practical obstacles such as difficulty in establishing nationality or the lack of a safe route of return can prevent removal.

210.   Subsection (3) allows the Secretary of State to revoke the indefinite leave of a person and that person's dependants in certain cases where a person is no longer a refugee – for example, by accepting the protection of the country of their nationality or establishing themselves in that country.. As those concerned will no longer require the protection of the United Kingdom, subsection (7) allows for administrative removal by amending section 10(1) of the 1999 Act.

211.   Subsections (5) and (6) provide that leave granted before the power comes into force may be revoked. In relation to subsections (1) and (2) but not (3) leave may also be revoked where the action which triggers revocation occurs before the power comes into force.

Section 77: No removal while claim for asylum pending

212. Section 77 replaces section 15 of the 1999 Act which provides that an asylum claimant may not be removed from or required to leave the United Kingdom before notice of the Secretary of State's decision on the claim is given. The new section only prohibits removals in accordance with a provision in the Immigration Acts, and subsection (4) allows removal directions or a deportation order to be given and other interim or preparatory action to be taken before notice of a decision on the claim has been given.

Section 78: No removal while appeal pending

213. Section 78 makes provision equivalent to that in Schedule 4 of the 1999 Act, which states that a person may not be removed from or required to leave the United Kingdom while he is in the country and his appeal is pending, as defined in section 104. Again, this only applies to removal or a requirement to leave under the Immigration Acts, and removal directions may be given or, subject to section 79, a deportation order may be made while the appeal is pending. Subsection (3) also allows other interim or preparatory action to be taken.

Section 79: Deportation order: appeal

214. Section 79 makes provision equivalent to section 63(2) of the 1999 Act and paragraph 18 of Schedule 4 to that Act which prevent a deportation order being made during the period allowed for appealing against the decision to make it or while such an appeal is pending. "Pending" is defined in section 104.

Section 80: Removal of asylum-seeker to third country

215. This provision replaces section 11 of the 1999 Act. The definition of standing arrangements is amended to ensure that any bilateral agreements on asylum returns with Member States outside of the Dublin Convention to which section 11 already applied, also will fall within this provision.

PART 5: IMMIGRATION AND ASYLUM APPEALS

Appeal to adjudicator
Section 81 and Schedule 4: Adjudicators

216. Section 81 sets out the criteria for the appointment of adjudicators by the Lord Chancellor and for functions to be assigned to the Chief Adjudicator, Deputy Chief Adjudicator, Regional Adjudicators and Deputy Regional Adjudicators. Subsection (1) requires the Lord Chancellor to appoint adjudicators to hear appeals under Part 5 of the Act. Subsection (2) states the qualifications or experience necessary for appointment. Subsection (3) requires the Lord Chancellor to appoint a Chief Adjudicator, and enables him to appoint a Deputy Chief Adjudicator, one or more Regional Adjudicators and one or more Deputy Regional Adjudicators. Subsection (4) requires the Chief Adjudicator to carry out such functions as the Lord Chancellor

may assign. Subsection (5) sets out the duties of the Deputy Chief Adjudicator. Subsection (6) sets out that Regional Adjudicators shall perform such functions as are assigned to them by the Chief Adjudicator. Subsection (7) sets out the duties of a Deputy Regional Adjudicator. Subsection (8) provides for Schedule 4 to have effect.

217.   Schedule 4 makes provision on the terms of office of, proceedings before, and payment arrangements for, adjudicators and their support staff. Paragraph 1 deals with the terms of office for adjudicators. Paragraph 2 requires the Chief Adjudicator to arrange for adjudicators to hear appeals and specifies that these must take place when and where the Lord Chancellor determines. Paragraph 3 enables the Chief Adjudicator to determine that a panel consisting of more than one adjudicator may deal with a particular appeal or category of appeal or appeal-related proceedings. Paragraph 4 requires adjudicators to carry out duties allocated by the Chief Adjudicator.

218.   Paragraph 5 of Schedule 4 enables the Lord Chancellor to appoint staff to support adjudicators. Paragraph 6 relates to the remuneration, allowances and expenses of adjudicators and their staff. Paragraph 7 concerns payment of compensation on ceasing to be an adjudicator in special circumstances.

Section 82: Right of appeal: general

219.   Section 82 and related sections differ considerably in structure from the earlier legislation on immigration appeals, in order to produce a clearer package of appeal rights. The scheme is based on the principle that there is one right of appeal against any of the listed "immigration decisions". Where multiple decisions would result in multiple rights of appeal these are subsumed into one appeal. All appealable grounds of appeal can be raised in that appeal (section 86). The requirement for a person to state all grounds for their application, see section 120, helps to ensure that all relevant issues are dealt with in one appeal. Exceptions and limitations restrict rights of appeal in certain circumstances and define which appeals can be exercised in the United Kingdom (sections 88 to 95).

220.   Subsection (2) lists the "immigration decisions" which attract rights of appeal. These are basically the same decisions that trigger a right of appeal under Part IV of the 1999 Act, but there is a new decision (revocation of indefinite leave under section 76 of the Act). The position relating to removal directions has been clarified. It is the initial immigration decision which may result in removal which attracts the right of appeal, not any consequential giving of directions to the carrier or re-giving of directions following an appeal or temporary suspension.

221.   Subsection(3) states that where a decision curtails a person's leave to enter or remain so that none remains, or revokes indefinite leave, the variation does not have effect during the period when an appeal may be brought or while an appeal is pending.

Section 83: Appeal: asylum claim

222.   Section 83 gives a right of appeal to an adjudicator on asylum grounds only (see section 84(3)) when an asylum claimant is refused asylum but granted leave to enter

or remain for more than a year. If periods of less than 12 months are given, the right of appeal arises when an aggregate of 12 months leave has been given since the decision to refuse asylum was taken. There is no right of appeal under section 82 for a person in this position and the purpose of this provision is to provide a specific single-issue asylum appeal.

Section 84: Grounds of appeal

223.   Section 84 lists in subsection (1) the grounds on which an appeal under section 82(1) can be brought. Listing the grounds in this way both illustrates what grounds are possible or acceptable and follows the categories of appeal set out in the earlier legislation, for example, immigration appeals, asylum appeals, human rights appeals and race relations appeals. What was a separate category of appeal is now simply a possible ground for the one appeal.

Section 85: Matters to be considered

224.   Section 85(1) provides that an appeal under section 82(1) shall be treated by an adjudicator as including an appeal against any decision where the person has a right of appeal under section 82(1). Thus it is not necessary for a person to lodge separate appeals if subject to different immigration decisions: all appealable decisions are to be subsumed in the one appeal.

225.   If a person makes a statement under section 120 in response to a requirement to state any additional grounds (the "one-stop warning"), the adjudicator must consider any of the matters raised in the statement, if these matters amount to a ground of appeal, as listed in section 84. It does not matter whether the statement is made before or after the appeal is commenced (subsections (2) and (3)).

226.   Subsection (4) allows the adjudicator to consider any evidence that he thinks is relevant to the substance of the decision, including any evidence which arises after the date of decision. The subsection also applies to appeals under section 83 where asylum has been refused but leave to remain granted. But subsection (4) does not apply to an appeal against the refusal of an entry clearance or a certificate of entitlement: in these cases the adjudicator can only consider the circumstances as they were at the time of the decision to refuse.

Section 86: Determination of Appeal

227.   This section describes what adjudicators are required to do in consideration of appeals under sections 82(1) or 83. Adjudicators will be required to determine any ground of appeal which is raised in response to any decision against which an appeal has been lodged or against which an appeal is to be treated as included by virtue of section 85(1). They must also determine any other matters which are raised which must be considered under section 85.

228.   Subsection (3) states that an adjudicator must allow an appeal if he thinks a relevant decision was not in accordance with the law or that a discretion should have been exercised differently. Otherwise, the appeal must be dismissed (subsection (5)). A

refusal to depart from the Immigration Rules does not count as the exercise of a discretion for this purpose (subsection (6)).

229.   Subsection (4) indicates that a decision that a person should be removed from the United Kingdom will not be regarded as unlawful if the decision to remove could have been lawfully made under another provision. Thus if the adjudicator comes to a different conclusion from the Secretary of State about the person's nationality or immigration status, but nevertheless considers that the decision to remove is correct on its merits, the appeal does not have to be allowed on a technicality and the process re-started.

Section 87: Successful appeal: direction

230.   Section 87 deals with directions which can be given by an adjudicator when allowing an appeal.   There is a power under subsection (1) for an adjudicator to give a direction for the purposes of giving an effect to his decision. Subsection (2) requires a decision-maker to act in accordance with any relevant direction. Subsection (3) provides that a direction shall not have effect while an appeal to the Tribunal or a further appeal could be brought, or has been brought and not been finally determined. Under subsection (4) the direction is treated as part of the adjudicator's determination.

Sections 88 to 99: Exceptions and limitations

231.   Sections 88 to 99 set out detailed provisions relating to exceptions and limitations on the general right of appeal as well as stating when appeals may be pursued in the United Kingdom (i.e. when they are "suspensive").   It should be noted that the exceptions do not generally prevent an appeal being brought on asylum, human rights or race discrimination grounds.

Section 88: Ineligibility

232.   Section 88 deals with cases where the application has been refused because the person (or a person on whom his application depends) does not meet a basic non-discretionary requirement of the Immigration Rules: thus any appeal based on the Rules could not succeed. An additional category (to those established in the 1999 Act) is subsection (2)(d), which prevents an appeal where the applicant wished to stay for a purpose not covered by the Immigration Rules. Some categories of application currently regarded as "concessions" outside the Rules will be incorporated into the Rules. An appeal may nevertheless be brought on asylum, human rights or race discrimination grounds.

Section 89: Visitor or student without entry clearance

233.   Section 89 retains the 1999 Act exceptions relating to a person without entry clearance who applies for leave to enter the United Kingdom at a port of entry as a visitor, a student (who has not enrolled on a course or has enrolled on a course that lasts less than six months) or a dependant of such a person. No appeal can be brought against a decision to refuse entry in these cases (subsection (2)), except on asylum, human rights or race discrimination grounds.

Section 90: Non-family visitor

234. Section 90 restricts appeals against the refusal of entry clearance for a visit to those cases involving a visit to a family member in the United Kingdom. But it does not prevent any other visit applicant who is refused entry clearance from appealing on asylum, race or human rights grounds. Subsections (2) and (3) provide for regulations to be made to define who are to be regarded as family members.

Section 91: Student

235. Section 91 retains the exceptions for appeals by students and their dependants who are refused entry clearance. There is no appeal if the person has not been accepted for a course, or has been accepted and the course lasts for less than six months. This section does not prevent appeals on race or human rights grounds.

Section 92: Appeal from within United Kingdom: general

236. Section 92 sets out the circumstances in which a person may appeal while he is in the United Kingdom, suspending any removal which might follow from the decision. While the appeal is pending a person who has made an asylum or human rights claim or European claim while in the United Kingdom may appeal while in the United Kingdom (subsection (4)). See sections 93 and 94 for cases where the appeal must be brought after the claimant has left the United Kingdom.

237. Other appeals will only be suspensive when made against certain types of decision (subsections (2) and (3)). These **include**: a decision to make a deportation order; a refusal of leave to enter at the port if the applicant holds an entry clearance or work permit; a decision relating to a person who applied for an extension of stay before his existing leave expired; and a decision to curtail a person's leave to enter or remain. Appeals against the refusal of a certificate of entitlement under section 10 and revocation of indefinite leave are also suspensive.

Section 93: Appeal from within United Kingdom: "third country" removal

238. Clause 93 is broadly similar to a provision in earlier legislation relating to cases where a certificate has been issued under section 11 or 12 of the 1999 Act (removal of asylum claimants to a "third country"). Under subsection (1) a person may not appeal under section 82(1) while in the United Kingdom if a certificate has been issued. If, however, the appellant has made a human rights claim which the Secretary of State has not certified as clearly unfounded, the person can appeal while in the United Kingdom (subsection (2)).

Section 94: Appeal from within the United Kingdom: unfounded human rights or asylum claim

239. This section applies to a right of appeal against an immigration decision (see section 82(1)). Where the person has made either an asylum claim or a human rights claim, or both, an appeal may not be brought while the person is in the United Kingdom by virtue of section 92(4) i.e. on the grounds that they have made an asylum or human rights claim, if the Secretary of State certifies that the claim or claims are clearly

unfounded.

240.   Subsection (3) provides that if the asylum or human rights claimant is entitled to reside in any of the States listed in subsection (4) then the claim shall be certified unless the Secretary of State is satisfied that it is not clearly unfounded. The States listed are all "EU accession states": Cyprus, the Czech Republic, Estonia, Hungary, Latvia, Lithuania, Malta, Poland, the Slovak Republic and Slovenia.

241.   Subsection (5) enables the Secretary of State, by order, to add a State, or part of a State to the list in subsection (4) if he is satisfied that there is in general no serious risk of persecution in the State or part State of persons entitled to reside there and that removal to that State will not in general contravene the United Kingdom's obligations under ECHR. Subsection (6) allows for a State or part State that has been added in accordance with subsection (5) to be removed, by order.

242.   Subsection (7) provides that an appeal may not be brought while the person is in the United Kingdom in reliance on section 92(4), if the Secretary of State certifies that it is intended to remove the applicant to a third country of which he is not a national and that there is no reason to suppose that his human rights will be breached in that country. Subsection (8) provides that a country which is named in the certificate to which it is intended to remove an applicant under subsection (7), is to be regarded as one where the applicant's rights under the Refugee Convention will be observed and from where he will not be sent to another country other than in accordance with the Convention.

243.   Subsection (9) provides that where a certificate is issued under this section an appeal that is made outside of the United Kingdom shall be considered as if the applicant had not been removed from this country.

Section 95: Appeal from outside United Kingdom: removal
244.   This provision prevents an appeal being lodged on asylum grounds by a person who is outside the United Kingdom. It does not apply when a person has been removed on the basis that their asylum claim has been certified under section 94: in that case the asylum appeal must necessarily be made from abroad.

Section 96: Earlier right of appeal
245.   Sections 96 and 120 set out the "one-stop" arrangements which prevent a person from seeking to appeal when they have already had an opportunity to put their case to an adjudicator. In all cases, the person will have been required to state any grounds for their application. The earlier legislation (section 73 of the 1999 Act) has been extended in a number of respects. This section covers situations where a person chooses not to appeal a decision but nevertheless makes a further claim or application; where a person withdraws or abandons an appeal but makes a further claim or application; and where a person chooses not to make a claim in response to a requirement under section 120 which would give rise to a right of appeal but has no right of appeal in respect of the matters he has actually put forward. The section also

makes it clearer that certification powers are, where the relevant conditions are met, also applicable where a further claim or application is made after leaving and returning to the United Kingdom.

246. Under subsection (1) no appeal can be brought on any ground against an otherwise appealable decision if the Secretary of State or immigration officer certifies that the person was notified of a right of appeal against another decision - whether or not any appeal was lodged or completed - and that in his opinion the person made their claim or application in order to delay removal, or the removal of a family member, and that in his opinion the person had no other legitimate purpose for making the claim or application. If an appeal has already been brought, the appeal may not be continued if a certificate is issued.

247. Subsection (2) prevents an appeal being brought if the Secretary of State or immigration officer certifies that a new decision relates to a ground which was raised on an earlier appeal, or should have been declared in response to an earlier requirement under section 120, or could have been raised at an appeal had the applicant chosen to exercise a right of appeal. If an appeal has already been brought, the appeal may not be continued if a certificate is issued.

248. Under subsection (3), where a further appeal right does arise, the Secretary of State or immigration officer may certify that certain grounds of appeal were already considered in an earlier appeal. The appellant is not then allowed to rely on those grounds.

249. Subsection (4) indicates that the word "notified" in subsection (1) means notified in accordance with regulations made under section 105. These "Notices" Regulations will set out the circumstances when rights of appeal are to be notified and require that information be given as to how to appeal and the assistance available.

250. Subsection (5) indicates that a claim or application or grounds of appeal can be certified if the person has left the United Kingdom and subsequently returned.

251. Subsection (6) ensures that appeals, or potential appeals, to the Special Immigration Appeals Commission are counted as appeals or potential appeals for the purposes of this section.

Section 97 National Security, &c.
252. Section 97 provides that where the Secretary of State certifies that a decision was taken on certain grounds (subsection (2)) or in reliance on certain information (subsection (3)), the person may not appeal under this Act. However, under the Special Immigration Appeals Commission Act 1997 they may appeal to the Special Immigration Appeals Commission (SIAC), the body set up specifically to deal with appeals where national security and other sensitive matters are a consideration.

Section 98: Other grounds of public good

253.   Section 98 prevents a person from appealing a refusal of leave to enter or refusal of entry clearance, or prevents such an appeal from continuing, where the Secretary of State has personally certified that the person's exclusion from the United Kingdom is conducive to the public good, or directed that the person be refused on that ground. Subsections (4) and (5) provide that this does not prevent the person appealing on human rights or race discrimination grounds, or from appealing refusal of leave to enter on asylum grounds.

Section 99: sections 96 to 98: appeal in progress

254.   This section provides for a pending appeal to lapse if it is certified under section 96(1) or (2), 97 or 98.

Appeal from adjudicator

Section 100 and Schedule 5: Immigration Appeal Tribunal

255.   Section 100 provides for the Tribunal to continue in being and gives effect to Schedule 5.

256.   Schedule 5 makes further provision about the Immigration Appeal Tribunal. Paragraph 1 requires the Lord Chancellor to appoint its members and paragraph 2 deals with certain terms of office. Paragraph 3 requires the Lord Chancellor to appoint as President a member who holds or has held high judicial office, and paragraph 4 requires him to appoint a legally-qualified member of the Tribunal as Deputy President and sets out his functions. Paragraph 5 requires the Tribunal to sit when and where the Lord Chancellor determines. Paragraphs 6 and 7 enable the Tribunal to sit in more than one division and enable the President to direct that certain cases or classes of case be decided by a single member or a set number of members, or legally qualified members.

257.   Paragraph 8 enables the Lord Chancellor to appoint staff for the Tribunal while paragraphs 9 and 10 concern remuneration and allowances for the Tribunal and its staff, Tribunal expenses, and compensation should a member leave in special circumstances. Paragraph 11 sets out the requirements for designation as a legally qualified member of the Tribunal.

Section 101: Appeal to Tribunal

258.   Subsection (1) provides an appeal with permission to the Tribunal against the adjudicator's decision on a point of law. Subsection (2) provides that a party to an application to the Tribunal for permission to appeal may apply to the High Court or, in Scotland, to the Court of Session, for a review of the Tribunal's decision on the ground that the Tribunal made an error of law. Subsection (3) provides that an application shall be determined by a single judge by reference only to written submissions. The judge may affirm or reverse the Tribunal's decision, and the judge's decision is final. Subsection (3) also provides that if, in an application to the High Court, the judge thinks the application had no merit he is required to issue a

certificate to this effect. Subsection (4) allows the Lord Chancellor to make an order to repeal the statutory review process set out in subsections (2) and (3). The order is subject to affirmative resolution.

Section 102: Decision

259. Subsection (1) sets out the options open to the Tribunal when determining an appeal: it may affirm the adjudicator's decision (subsection (1)(a)), make any decision which the adjudicator could have made (subsection (1)(b)), remit it to an adjudicator (subsection (1)(c)), affirm any directions made by the adjudicator under section 87, or vary or give any direction which the adjudicator could have given.

260. Subsections (2) and (3) govern the evidence the Tribunal may consider. This is on the same basis as evidence which may be considered by an adjudicator under section 85 (4) and (5). Subsection (4) enables the Tribunal, in remitting an appeal to an adjudicator, to require the adjudicator to determine the appeal in accordance with its directions, or to take additional evidence so that the case may come back to the Tribunal for determination.

Section 103: Appeal from Tribunal

261. Subsection (1) provides that where the Tribunal determines an appeal, under section 101, a party to the appeal may bring a further appeal to the Court of Appeal on a point of law. Where the original decision of the adjudicator was made in Scotland, a party to the appeal may bring a further appeal to the Court of Session on a point of law. Subsection (2) provides that such a further appeal may be brought only with the permission of the Tribunal. If the Tribunal refuses permission, permission may be sought from the Court of Appeal or, in Scotland, the Court of Session.

Procedure
Section 104: Pending appeal

262. Section 104 makes provision equivalent to section 58 of the 1999 Act. It defines when an appeal under section 82(1) is pending, during which time the appellant is generally protected from enforcement of the consequences of a decision. An appeal is pending from the time it is instituted (in accordance with Procedure Rules under section 106). It remains pending until the time limit for taking it further expires or until it has been finally determined, withdrawn or abandoned. An appeal while the appellant is in the United Kingdom ceases to be pending if the person leaves the United Kingdom or is granted leave to enter or remain here (subsection (4)). In some circumstances (those specified in subsection (5)) the making of a deportation order brings appeals to an end. It is assumed that the relevant issues will have been addressed during the course of any appeal against the decision to deport the person concerned.

263. Subsection (3) now makes it clear that if the Tribunal remits an appeal to an adjudicator, its determination is not a final determination for this purpose, so the appeal remains pending.

264. The section does not apply to appeals under section 83 where leave to remain of more than 12 months has been granted to a person refused asylum.

Section 105: Notice of immigration decision

265. Section 105 makes provision similar to paragraph 1(1) of Schedule 4 to the 1999 Act, concerning regulations governing the service of appealable decisions. Regulations may be made requiring written notice to be given of an immigration decision within the terms of section 82. When the decision is appealable the notice must declare the right of appeal and give details of how it may be exercised. Subsection (3) enables the Notices Regulations to make provision for service of the notice, including presumptions - this might include, for example, provision for service where a person has absconded and no address is known.

Section 106: Rules

266. Section 106 makes provision similar to and expands upon paragraphs 3, 4 and 8 of Schedule 4 to the 1999 Act. Subsection (1) of section 106 allows the Lord Chancellor to make appeals procedure rules that regulate the exercise of the right of appeal in Part 5 of this Act and prescribe the procedure to be followed in connection with proceedings. Subsection (2) sets out particular matters that must or may be included in the rules. It clarifies the content and effect of paragraph 4 of Schedule 4 to the 1999 Act and provides that rules may make provision about the grant of bail (contained in the Immigration Act 1971). Subsection (3) introduces new measures which enable the rules to include provisions about costs powers for the adjudicator and the Tribunal. Subsections (4) and (5) re-enact paragraph 8 of Schedule 4 to the 1999 Act, which makes it an offence to fail to give evidence or produce a document without reasonable excuse when required to do so by the rules.

Section 107: Practice Directions

267. Section 107 enables practice directions to be given by the President of the Tribunal and the Chief Adjudicator.

Section 108: Forged document: proceedings in private

268. Section 108 makes provision equivalent to paragraph 6 of Schedule 4 to the 1999 Act which enables an adjudicator, following an allegation that relevant documents are forged, to hold further proceedings in private where to do otherwise would not be in the public interest. The class of document which may be relevant has been extended since many types of document may be submitted in evidence and these may rely on sophisticated technologies. The security features, ways of forging or defeating them and forgery detection methods should not normally be divulged to the public.

General

Section 109: European Union and European Economic Area

269. This section allows the Secretary of State to make regulations that may provide for an appeal against an immigration decision taken in respect of a person who has, or who claims to have, a right under any of the Community Treaties. Subsection (2) states that these Regulations may apply this Act or the Special Immigration Appeals

Commission Act 1997, with or without modification. Subsection (3) defines that an immigration decision for this section is one about a person's entitlement to enter, remain or one about a person's removal from the United Kingdom.

Section 110: Grants

270. Section 110 enables the Secretary of State to make grants to voluntary organisations which assist, advise or give other services with regard to the welfare of those who have a right of appeal under this Part of the Act. Grants may be conditional, including conditions as to repayment in certain circumstances.

Section 111: Monitor of certification of claims as unfounded

271. Section 111 requires the Secretary of State to appoint a person to monitor the use of the powers under sections 94(2) and 115(1) (which relate to certifying asylum and human rights claims as clearly unfounded). The person appointed must produce a report once a year to the Secretary of State who must in turn lay a copy of that report before Parliament. The Secretary of State may also request the appointed person to make additional reports. The person may not be employed within a government department.

Section 112: Regulations, &c.

272. Section 112 is a general provision regarding regulations and rules for this Part of the Act. They will be negative resolution statutory instruments, except orders made under sections 94(5), 101(4) and 115(8), which are affirmative orders.

Section 113: Interpretation

273. Subsection (1) defines certain common terms which are used throughout Part 5. The definitions of "asylum claim" and "human rights claim" reflect the intention that a claim can only be made in person at a designated place.

274. Subsection (2) ensures that references to varying leave to enter or remain do not cover decisions taken in relation to conditions of leave. For example, appeal rights do not accrue from a decision to refuse to allow a person to take employment if they are still permitted to remain here.

Section 114: Repeal

275. Subsection(1) repeals Part IV of the 1999 Act, which this Part replaces. Subsection (2) gives effect to Schedule 6 (transitional provisions). Subsection (3) gives effect to Schedule 7 (consequential amendments).

Section 115: Appeal from within the United Kingdom: unfounded human rights or asylum claim: transitional provision

276. Section 115 applies similar provisions to those in Section 94 to appeals against refusals of asylum and human rights claims which are clearly unfounded and which are made in the transitional period between the granting of Royal Assent to this Act and the coming into force of the rest of Part 5. It therefore applies to appeals under

Part IV of the Immigration and Asylum Act 1999.

277.   Subsection (1) provides that an appeal cannot be brought while in the United Kingdom under sections 65 or 69 of the 1999 Act if the Secretary of State certifies that the appeal relates to an asylum or human rights claim which is clearly unfounded and where the individual does not have another right of appeal while in the United Kingdom under Part IV of the 1999 Act.

278.   Subsection (2) provides that a person may not bring an asylum appeal while in the United Kingdom under section 69 or raise a question at an appeal under section 77 of the 1999 Act, if the Secretary of State certifies that it is proposed to remove him to a third country of which he is not a national and where there is no reason to believe that his human rights will be breached. Subsection (3) provides that a person may not bring a human rights appeal under section 65 of the 1999 Act if the same criteria as in subsection (2) are met.

279.   Subsection (4) states that, in deciding whether a person who has been issued with a certificate under subsections (2) or (3) may be removed from the United Kingdom, the country specified in the certificate is to be regarded as one where the individual's rights against persecution under the Refugee Convention will be met and one from where he will not be sent to another country other than in accordance with the Convention.

280.   Subsection (5) provides that where a certificate is issued under this section, and an appeal or question under sections 65, 69 or 77 of the 1999 Act is made outside of the United Kingdom, the appeal will be considered as if the appellant had not been removed from this country.

281.   Subsection (6) provides that when a person who is entitled to reside in any of the countries listed in subsection (7) makes an asylum or human rights claim, then the claim is to be certified unless the Secretary of State is satisfied that it is not clearly unfounded. The states listed are all "EU accession states": Cyprus, the Czech Republic, Estonia, Hungary, Latvia, Lithuania, Malta, Poland, the Slovak Republic and Slovenia.

282.   Subsection (8) empowers the Secretary of State, by order, to add a State, or part of a State to the list in subsection (7) if he is satisfied that there is in general no serious risk of persecution in the State or part State of persons entitled to reside there and that removal to that State will not in general contravene our obligations under ECHR. Subsection (9) allows for a State or part State that has been added in accordance with subsection (8) to be removed, by order.

Section 116: Special Immigration Appeals Commission: Community Legal Service
283.   Section 116 brings proceedings before the Special Immigration Appeals Commission within the scope of the Community Legal Service, created under the Access to Justice

Act 1999.

Section 117: Northern Ireland appeals: legal aid

284.   This section amends Part 1 of Schedule 1 to the Legal Aid, Advice and Assistance (Northern Ireland) Order 1981 (S.I. 1981/228 (N.I. 8)) (proceedings for which legal aid may be given under Part II of that Order) to bring proceedings before the Immigration Adjudicators, the Immigration Appeal Tribunal   (the Immigration Appellate Authority) and the Special Immigration Appeals Commission (SIAC) within the scope of legal aid in Northern Ireland.

PART 6 - IMMIGRATION PROCEDURE

Applications
Section 118: Leave pending decision on variation application

285.   Section 118 replaces section 3C of the 1971 Act, which ensures that persons who make an application for leave "in time", that is before their current leave expires, are protected from becoming overstayers while their application is outstanding and while an appeal against a full refusal can be made in time or is pending.   The earlier provision made no allowance for leave extended by this section to expire when an application was withdrawn or the applicant left the United Kingdom without formally withdrawing the application.   These situations are now covered in subsection (2)(a) and (3) of the substituted section 3C.

Section 119: Deemed leave on cancellation of notice

286.   Section 119 amends paragraph 6(3) of Schedule 2 to the Immigration Act 1971. When a notice refusing leave to enter is cancelled the Immigration Officer may, instead of granting the person either indefinite or limited leave to enter, require him to submit to further examination.   Therefore, when notifying cancellation of a notice of refusal of leave to enter the Immigration Officer is not obliged to make a further decision immediately, in order to avoid deemed leave being granted, but can instead notify the person that, for example, they will be interviewed or be given the opportunity to provide further written evidence before a decision is made to grant or refuse leave to enter.

Section 120: Requirement to state additional grounds for application

287.   Section 120 replaces and extends the application of the one-stop notice in section 75 of the 1999 Act. There is now no limitation on the category of applicant on whom the requirement to state grounds for application and the "one-stop warning" can be served and IND has the operational freedom to serve it at any appropriate point in the process.

288.   Subsection (1) applies the section to people who have made an application to enter or remain in the United Kingdom and to people in respect of whom a relevant decision has been or may be taken without an application being made: for example where it is

proposed to remove someone as an illegal entrant.

289.   Subsection (2) states that when served with a "notice in writing" the person is required to state all his reasons for wishing to enter or remain in the UK, and any grounds on which IND should be obliged to let him enter or remain here, and any grounds on which he should not be removed. If he does not do so, any attempt to raise such grounds later on may lead to certification under section 96 with the effect that there can be no appeal against the decision, or that those grounds cannot be raised in connection with a further appeal.

290.   Subsection (3) indicates that a statement made in response to a requirement and one-stop warning does not have to repeat what the applicant has already said in his application.

Section 121: Compliance with procedure

291.   Section 121 amends section 31A of the 1971 Act (as inserted by the 1999 Act). This clarifies the consequences if an application to enter or remain in the UK is not made on a prescribed form or in a prescribed manner. Regulations may provide for the consequences of failure to comply with specified requirements, including that it invalidates an application, does not invalidate an application or invalidates an application in certain circumstances.

Work permits

Section 122: Fee for work permit, &c

292.   Section 122 gives the Secretary of State the power to charge for the consideration of applications for immigration employment documents, including work permits and letters of permission issued in-country, which give authority to work and which underpin employment-related leave to enter or remain.

293.   Subsection (3) establishes that the details of charging are to be set out in regulations. These regulations may make different provision in relation to different types or classes of applications. Such variation would allow, for example, different charges (including exemptions) to be introduced according to the type of application or the nature of the employer. Subsection (4) allows such regulations to specify that particular payment arrangements may apply in relation to certain applications.

Section 123: Advice about work permit, &c

294.   Section 123 inserts a new paragraph into subsection (1) and a new subsection (3) in section 82 of the 1999 Act. The effect is that applications for an immigration employment document will become a "relevant matter" for the purposes of the regulatory scheme established by Part V of the 1999 Act. This means that anyone who provides advice and/or services regarding work permit applications or any other document relating to the employment of a foreign national in the course of a business will be subject to the regulatory scheme established by Part V of the 1999 Act and administered by the Immigration Services Commissioner.

Authority-to-carry scheme

Section 124: Authority to carry

295.   Section 124 makes provision for the Authority – to-carry (ATC) scheme. This will enable the Secretary of State to operate a scheme, which requires carriers to seek authority for bringing passengers to the United Kingdom. It is envisaged that a scheme or schemes will require them to do so by checking the details of passengers travelling to the United Kingdom against information held on a Home Office database to confirm that they pose no known immigration or security risk and to confirm that their documents are in order. This will take place before the passenger embarks for the United Kingdom.

296.   Subsection (1) allows the Secretary of State to make regulations requiring a carrier who brings a person to the United Kingdom to pay a penalty if they do not seek authority to carry a person, or if they carry a person even though authority has been refused, when required to do so.

297.   Subsection (3) provides that ATC may be applied to any class of carrier or passenger and subsection (4) allows the Secretary of State to operate different ATC schemes for different purposes.

298.   Subsections (6) and (7) provide that the regulations made under this section may mirror or amend carrier's liability legislation, which concerns people arriving in the United Kingdom without valid travel documents or visas.

299.   Subsection (8) provides that a decision as to whether to grant authority under the scheme does not indicate whether the person is entitled or permitted to enter the United Kingdom.

Evasion of Procedure

Section 125 and Schedule 8: Carriers' liability

300.   The section provides that Schedule 8 shall have effect. Paragraph 2 of Schedule 8 amends section 32 of the 1999 Act, which relates to the penalty payable for carriage of a clandestine entrant into the United Kingdom.

301.   Sub-paragraph (2) introduces provisions into the 1999 Act which are currently contained in the Regulations that extend the penalty regime to rail freight wagons (S.I. 2001/280 as amended). Thus a clandestine entrant, as defined by section 32(1) of the 1999 Act, includes someone who arrives in the United Kingdom concealed in a vehicle, ship, aircraft or rail freight wagon and who claims, or indicates that he intends to seek, asylum in the United Kingdom, or who evades, or attempts to evade immigration control.

302.   Sub-paragraph (3) amends section 32 so that it provides that a person responsible for a clandestine entrant may be held individually liable to pay a penalty in respect of the clandestine entrant and any person concealed with that clandestine entrant. The Secretary of State may impose, in respect of each clandestine entrant, an individual

penalty of no more than a prescribed maximum on each responsible person whilst limiting the total combined amount to a prescribed maximum in respect of each clandestine entrant. Rather than being held jointly and severally liable, as currently provided for in the 1999 Act, each responsible person will be liable for his own penalty.

303. However, further to the amendments made by sub-paragraph (4), where a penalty is imposed on a driver who is the employee of the vehicle's owner or hirer, the driver's employer, as well as the driver, will be liable for payment of that penalty.

304. The amendments made by sub-paragraph (6) mean that where the clandestine entrant is concealed in a freight train, the responsible person is the train operator who was responsible for certifying the relevant train as fit to travel to the United Kingdom or (in the case of a freight shuttle wagon) the operator of the shuttle train of which the wagon forms part.

305. Pursuant to amendments made by sub-paragraph (8), where a person is responsible in more than one capacity, for example, as both the owner and driver of a vehicle, a separate penalty may be imposed on him in respect of each capacity.

306. Paragraph 3 creates a new section 32A of the 1999 Act introducing a new code in relation to setting the level of the penalty.

307. Subsection (1) of the new section requires the Secretary of State to issue a code of practice specifying the matters to be considered in determining the amount of a penalty. Under subsection (2) the Secretary of State must have regard to the code and any other relevant matters when imposing a penalty and when considering a notice of objection against a penalty.

308. By subsections (3) to (6), the Secretary of State is required to lay a draft of the code before Parliament before issuing it and then may bring the code into operation by order. The Secretary of State may subsequently revise and reissue the code.

309. Paragraph 6 amends section 34 of the 1999 Act in relation to the defences to the imposition of a penalty under section 32 of that Act.

310. Sub-paragraph (4) inserts a new subsection (3A) which creates a defence for rail freight operators in circumstances where the operator knew, or suspected that a clandestine entrant was, or might be, concealed in the rail freight wagon, having boarded the train or shuttle train after it had begun its journey to the United Kingdom, and the operator could not stop the train or shuttle train without endangering safety.

311. Paragraph 7 amends section 35 of the 1999 Act by clarifying the procedure for the issuing of the penalty notice and objecting to the issue of a penalty notice.

312. Amendments made by sub-paragraph (3) mean that a responsible person may give

notice of objection to the Secretary of State in the required form and within the prescribed period if he objects on the grounds that he is not liable to the imposition of a penalty or that the amount of the penalty is too high. The Secretary of State may then affirm, vary or cancel the penalty and inform the objector of his decision within a prescribed or agreed period. If the penalty is increased, a new penalty notice must be issued.

313.   Paragraph 8 of the Schedule introduces a new statutory right of appeal against the imposition of a penalty in a new section 35A of the 1999 Act. A person may contest both liability to a penalty and the level of the penalty in the county court (or equivalent court in Scotland). The court may cancel or reduce the penalty, or dismiss the appeal. The appeal will be a re-hearing of the Secretary of State's decision to impose a penalty and the court hearing the appeal must have regard to any code of practice relating to the level of penalty in effect at the time of the appeal, the code of practice relating to prevention of clandestine entrants in effect when the penalty was issued and any other relevant matters (which may include matters of which the Secretary of State was unaware). An appeal may be brought whether or not a notice of objection has been given or the penalty has been increased or reduced under the objection procedure.

314.   Paragraph 9 amends section 36 of the 1999 Act which relates to the detention of vehicles.

315.   Sub-paragraph (3) provides the power to detain a transporter for up to 24 hours pending a decision on whether to issue a penalty notice, pending the issuing of a penalty notice, or pending a decision whether to detain a transporter under section 36(1). This is to take account of the time it may take in some instances to complete the necessary enquiries to establish the identity of those who are potentially liable to pay a penalty, to determine the level of any penalty to be imposed, and to consider whether there is a significant risk that the penalty will not be paid if the transporter is not detained under section 36(1).

316.   Paragraph 10 inserts a new section 36A into the 1999 Act which provides the power to detain a transporter where a person to whom a penalty notice has been issued fails to pay the penalty before the specified date. Under this power any transporter used, in connection with his business, by the person to whom the penalty notice has been issued (provided that this is the owner or hirer of the transporter, or their employee at the time the penalty notice was issued) may be detained. Detention cannot take place if an appeal against the penalty is pending or can be brought. A detained transporter will be released if the penalty and any connected expenses are paid.

317.   Paragraph 11 amends section 37 of the 1999 Act which enables a person to apply to a court to have their transporter released.

318.   The amendment made by sub-paragraph (4) removes the requirement for a person, when applying to the court for the release of a transporter that has been detained in

accordance with section 36(1), to show a compelling need for its release. A transporter may be released if the court considers that a satisfactory security has been tendered, that there is no significant risk that the penalty and any connected expenses will not be paid, or that there is a significant doubt as to whether the penalty is payable.

319. Sub-paragraph (5) inserts new subsections (3A) and (3B) which provide that a court may also release a transporter detained under new sections 36A and 36(1) if a penalty notice was not issued to the owner or an employee of his or if the court considers it right to release the transporter. A transporter may also be released under new section 36A if the court considers that the detention was unlawful.

320. The amendment made by sub-paragraph (6) means that the power of sale under section 37(4) may only be exercised when no appeal against the penalty is pending or can be brought or with the consent of the owner.

321. Paragraph 13 substitutes a new section 40 of the 1999 Act. This provides for the charge imposed on carriers in respect of passengers arriving in the United Kingdom without proper documents. The owners of ships and aircraft will continue to be liable to a charge of £2,000 in respect of an individual who arrives in the United Kingdom and fails to produce the required documents. The owners and operators of road passenger vehicles will no longer be liable to a charge but there is a power for the Secretary of State to apply the section by order to passengers arriving by train.

322. A new section 40A sets out the procedures for notification of and objection to the penalty. The charge notice and notice of objections must contain certain information and follow a prescribed form. The Secretary of State will determine whether or not to cancel the charge within a prescribed or agreed period.

323. A new section 40B also provides a statutory right of appeal by which a carrier may contest his liability to a charge in the county court (or equivalent court in Scotland). The appeal will be a rehearing of the Secretary of State's decision to impose a charge and may be determined having regard to matters of which the Secretary of State was unaware. The court may cancel the charge or dismiss the appeal. An appeal may be brought whether or not a notice of objection has been given under the objection procedure.

324. Paragraph 14 removes the power to detain vehicles under section 40.

325. Amendments to Schedule 1 (sale of transporter) made by paragraph 16 mean that where the owner of a transporter is a party to an application for leave to sell it, in determining whether to give leave the court will consider the extent of any hardship likely to be caused by sale, the extent to which the owner is responsible under the penalty notice and any other relevant matters.

Provision of information by traveller

Section 126 : Physical data: compulsory provision

326.   This section supplements the current power to fingerprint and gather data from persons subject to immigration control, which is contained in sections 141 to 146 of the 1999 Act. Subsections (1) and (2) enable the Secretary of State to provide by regulations that a person who makes an application for a visa or entry clearance, or for leave to enter or remain (including variation of such leave) will be required to provide data specified in the regulations when making such an application, or to provide on demand such information to an "authorised person", who is enabled by the regulations to collect such data (for example, an entry clearance officer or immigration officer). The data that may be required extends to external physical characteristics, including features of the iris and any other part of the eye. By virtue of subsection (3), the power does not extend to those persons to whom section 141 of the 1999 Act contemporaneously applies. These persons continue to be covered by sections 141 to 146 of that Act.

327.   Subsections (4) to (8) make further provision about the content of the regulations. In particular, regulations may specify the form in which "data" should be provided and the means by which data may be obtained. They may also require persons authorised by the regulations to require the provision of data to have regard to any specified code of practice, or provisions thereof, that is in force under specified Police and Criminal Evidence legislation. The regulations may make provision for the use and retention of information provided, which may permit the use of information for specified non-immigration purposes. The regulations may also specify the consequences of an applicant failing to provide the requisite data, which may include the application in question being treated as invalid or refused. Additionally the requirements of the regulations can be specified to apply to certain cases or circumstances or to apply to all applications generally. There is no power to arrest persons who refuse to provide the data or to use reasonable force as remains the case for those covered by sections 141 to 146 of the 1999 Act. Regulations must provide for the destruction of data some 10 years from the date of recording of that data (unless another date is specified in the regulations for this purpose) and ensure that proper safeguards are in place when collecting data from those under the age of 16.

Section 127: Physical data: voluntary provision

328.   Under this section the Secretary of State may operate a scheme that enables people voluntarily to provide data of the type covered by section 126 with a view to assisting and accelerating their entry into the United Kingdom. By virtue of subsection (2), regulations made under this clause may impose or permit imposition of a charge on participants and may provide for safeguards regarding the use and retention of data.

Section 128: Data collection under Immigration and Asylum Act 1999

329.   This section amends section 144 of the 1999 Act to clarify that features of the iris or any other part of the eye come within the scope of external physical characteristics. This confirms that iris scans may be prescribed under section 144 of the 1999 Act and ensures that section 144 of that Act is interpreted in line with section 126. This section also ensures that those exercising powers taken under section 144 of the 1999

Act may be obliged to have regard to any specified code of practice, or (possibly modified) provisions thereof, that is in force under specified Police and Criminal Evidence legislation. Those collecting data under section 126 may also be required to have regard to such codes or provisions thereof.

Disclosure of information by public authority

Section 129: Local authority

330. This section provides that where the Secretary of State reasonably suspects that a person has committed a specified offence under the 1971 Act and is, or has been resident in a local authority area, the Secretary of State may require that local authority to provide information for the purpose of locating that person. It further provides that local authorities must comply with such a requirement.

Section 130: Inland Revenue

331. This section provides that the Commissioners of Inland Revenue may supply the Secretary of State with information for the purpose of establishing a person's whereabouts if the Secretary of State reasonably suspects that person does not have leave to be in the United Kingdom ; does not have permission to work; that he has worked in breach of conditions of leave or temporary admission. The Inland Revenue may also provide information to the Secretary of State for the purpose of determining whether an applicant for naturalisation under the British Nationality Act 1981 is of good character and for verifying whether a sponsored entry clearance applicant meets the maintenance and accommodation requirements of the Immigration Rules.

Section 131: Police, &c

332. Section 20 of the 1999 Act provides for information to be supplied to the Secretary of State by a number of bodies for immigration or other specified purposes. This section enables those bodies (including chief officers of police, the National Criminal Intelligence Service and HM Customs & Excise) to supply information to assist the Secretary of State in determining whether a person who has applied for naturalisation as a British citizen satisfies the "good character" requirements of the BNA 1981. Such information may include evidence of convictions.

Section 132: Supply of document, &c. to Secretary of State

333. Section 132 extends the scope of section 20 of the Immigration and Asylum Act 1999 to allow a person to whom the section applies who comes across physical objects, such as documents or replica immigration stamps, to pass them to the Secretary of State for immigration purposes.

334. Subsection (4) allows the Secretary of State to retain or dispose of documents or articles which are passed to him under this section.

Section 133: Medical inspectors

335. This section authorises port medical inspectors and staff working under their direction to disclose information to health service bodies for specific medical purposes. The information that can be disclosed is set out at subsection (2). The permitted purposes

of such disclosure are specified at subsection (3). "Health service body" is defined at subsection (4).

Disclosure of information by private person
Section 134: Employer

336. This section provides for the Secretary of State, where he has reasonable suspicion that a person has committed a specified immigration offence, including an offence in relation to earnings under the national asylum support arrangements, to require that person's employer to disclose information about that person's whereabouts, earnings or employment history. The provision applies to employers and to employment agencies hiring out the services of staff, whether those staff are self-employed, employed by the employment agency, or employed by a third party employer.

Section 135: Financial institution

337. This section provides for the Secretary of State to require a financial institution, such as a bank or building society, to supply information about a person whom the Secretary of State reasonably suspects of making a dishonest representation so as to commit a specified offence in relation to the national asylum support arrangements. To require information the Secretary of State must also reasonably suspect that the institution has the information and that it is relevant to the offence.

Section 136: Notice

338. This section sets out the form in which a requirement under sections 134 or 135 must be made, and what is required of an employer or financial institution in response to such a request. The request must be made in writing and must specify the information required, the manner in which it is to be provided and the time limit for replying, which must be at least 10 working days from receipt of the request. Within that time limit, the person on whom the notice is served must provide the information.

Section 137: Disclosure of information: offences

339. A person who without reasonable excuse does not comply with a request made under section 136(3) (which would include a person who falsely denies having the information requested) commits an offence punishable with a maximum penalty of a fine or three months imprisonment or both.

Section 138: Offence by body

340. The offence at section 137 may be committed by a natural or legal person, including a body corporate, such as a company. This section provides that where an offence under section 137 is committed by a body corporate, an officer of that body (which may include a manager, director, secretary or member) will have committed an offence if it is proved that the offence was committed with his consent or connivance, or was due to his neglect. The section also provides for liability of partners in a firm, making special provision for limited partnerships.

Section 139: Privilege against self-incrimination

341. This section provides that information provided by a person under sections 134 and 135 cannot be used in evidence in criminal proceedings against that person, except in proceedings for an offence under section 137.

Immigration Services
Section 140: Immigration Services Commissioner

342. Subsection (1) inserts a sub-paragraph in paragraph 7 of Schedule 5 to the 1999 Act to clarify that the Immigration Services Commissioner ("the Commissioner") may exercise his existing powers of entry when investigating a matter on his own initiative. These powers may be exercised to the same extent and in relation to the same matters as would be the case if the Commissioner was investigating a complaint made to him by a third party.

343. Subsection (2) inserts a new paragraph in Schedule 6 to the 1999 Act which enables the Commissioner to vary an adviser's registration during the period of an extant registration at any time without charge. Subsection (3) enables any decision made by the Immigration Services Commissioner in this way to be appealed to the Immigration Services Tribunal.

Section 141: EEA ports: juxtaposed controls

344. This section provides for a power that would allow the UK to operate immigration and other frontier controls at an EEA ferry port (such as Calais), for the purposes of giving effect to an international agreement. In addition, it would allow the Secretary of State to make any necessary legislative arrangements to accommodate French immigration control in UK ports (such as Dover).

345. Subsections (1) and (2) contain a power for the Secretary of State to make an order for the purpose of giving effect to an international agreement which concerns immigration control at an EEA port (which may also cover other frontier controls such as police and customs). The order may include any provision likely to facilitate implementation of that agreement.

346. Subsection (3) lists particular matters which may be included in a future order. .For example an order may specify that particular laws of England and Wales have effect (with or without modification) in that part of the EEA where immigration and other frontier controls are being carried out by UK officials. An order may also modify or even disapply UK legislation in order to allow officers from other countries to perform their functions on UK territory

347. Subsection (3)(f) provides that an order may make provision conferring a function, which may be discretionary and may be on a government officer of a State other than the UK.

348. Subsection (3)(g) states that an order may create or extend the application of an offence and subsections (3)(h) and (i) provide that an order may impose penalties or require payments of a fee, (for example a fee for processing a particular type of

immigration application).

349. Subsection (3)(j) states that an order may contain provision about enforcement, including conferring powers of arrest, detention or removal from or to a place.

350. Subsection (3)(k) allows an order to confer jurisdiction on a court.

351. Subsections (3)(l) and (m) provide for an order to confer immunity or provide for indemnity or compensation.

352. Subsection (3)(n) allows an order to make provision requiring , inter alia, UK port authorities to co-operate with or provide facilities for French officers to carry out their functions. It includes the power to require such facilities at no charge.

353. Finally, subsection 3(o) allows an order to make provision about the disclosure of information.

354. Subsection (5) states that the Secretary of State must consult with such persons as he considers appropriate before making an order under this section. Further, an order must be made by statutory instrument, which must be laid before and approved by both Houses of Parliament.

Section 142: Advisory panel on country information

355. The Act makes provision for the establishment of an advisory panel on country information.

356. Country information means information about the countries of origin of asylum seekers. The Immigration and Nationality Directorate compiles information regarding the political situation as well as human rights issues on the 35 countries that produce the highest numbers of asylum seekers to the UK. Their purpose is to document what is known about the countries in a way that might be relevant to making a decision on an asylum application.

357. The advisory panel will provide scrutiny and oversight of the quality and content of the country reports and review the methodology used in their compilation.

PART 7: OFFENCES

Substance
Section 143: Assisting unlawful immigration, &c.

358. Under section 25(1) of the 1971 Act it is an offence for someone to be knowingly concerned in making or carrying out arrangements for securing or facilitating the entry into the UK of an illegal entrant or (if done for gain) an asylum-seeker. It is also an offence knowingly to assist a person to obtain leave to remain in the United Kingdom by deception. The maximum penalty for these offences is 10 years

imprisonment and/or an unlimited fine. Where someone is convicted on indictment of an offence of assisting entry, the court can order the forfeiture of any ship, aircraft or vehicle used to commit the offence. (In the case of ships and aircraft this power is limited to vessels below a certain tonnage and aircraft below a certain operating weight (see section 25(7) of the 1971 Act).) The offence of assisting entry includes acts done outside the United Kingdom by a British citizen, a British Dependant Territories citizen, a British Overseas citizen, a British subject or a British protected person.

359. Under section 25(2) of the 1971 Act it is an offence to "harbour" an illegal entrant, a person who stays longer than allowed by their leave or a person who fails to observe another condition of their leave. The maximum penalty for this offence is 6 months imprisonment and/or a fine of £5,000.

360. Section 143 repeals section 25 of the 1971 Act and replaces it with four new sections (sections 25, 25A and 25B and 25C). Section 25 makes it an offence knowingly to facilitate someone to breach the laws of *any* Member State, not just the United Kingdom. This is a measure required to enable the United Kingdom to comply with Article 27 of the Schengen Convention, and will also assist compliance with a European Directive defining the facilitation of unauthorised entry, transit and residence and its associated Framework Decision, which will replace that Article. The maximum penalty for the offence has been increased to 14 years' imprisonment or an unlimited fine or both. There is no longer a separate offence of "harbouring". This conduct is now included as part of the general offence.

361. United Kingdom courts continue to have jurisdiction over acts of "assistance" given by certain classes of person outside the United Kingdom. The list has been expanded to include British Nationals (Overseas). "British National (Overseas)" is a form of British Nationality created by the Hong Kong Act 1985. Until 1997, British Nationals (Overseas) were also British Dependent Territories citizens and could be prosecuted for "assistance" given outside the United Kingdom on this basis. When they ceased to be British Dependent Territories citizens, they could no longer be prosecuted for such assistance. Their inclusion restores the pre-July 1997 position.

362. New Section 25A reproduces the offence which is presently section 25(1)(b) of the 1971 Act (namely, helping an asylum-seeker to enter the United Kingdom where this is done for gain). New section 25B makes it an offence to assist entry to the United Kingdom by a European citizen in breach of a deportation or exclusion order. New section 25C confers the same powers on courts to order the forfeiture of ships, aircraft and vehicles as exist presently, but extends the definition of an illegal entrant to include passengers trafficked contrary to the new offence in section 145 of this Act.

Section 144: Section 143: consequential amendments
363. This amends and renumbers the current section 25A of the 1971 Act which allows a vehicle, ship or aircraft which may be liable to forfeiture to be detained following a person's arrest, and makes consequential amendments to immigration officers' powers

of arrest, search and entry. Amendments in Schedule 7 replace the references in Schedules 2, 4 and 5 to the Proceeds of Crime Act 2002 to an offence under the present section 25(1) with references to offences under the new sections 25, 25A and 25B.

Section 145: Traffic in prostitution

364. Section 145 creates a criminal offence of trafficking people into, or out of, the United Kingdom for the purpose of controlling them in prostitution. A person commits the offence if he arranges for a person to enter or leave the United Kingdom and he intends to control them in prostitution there or elsewhere, or he believes another person is likely to control them in prostitution anywhere in the world. The offence is also committed if a person arranges travel within the United Kingdom if he believes that the passenger has been brought into the United Kingdom in order to be controlled in prostitution there or elsewhere and he intends to control them in prostitution, or believes another person is likely to do so, anywhere in the world. Controlling someone in prostitution means exercising control, direction or influence over a prostitute's movements in a way that shows he is aiding, abetting or compelling prostitution.

365. The offence is triable either summarily or on indictment. The maximum penalty on indictment is 14 years imprisonment, or an unlimited fine, or both.

366. Traffic in prostitution is designated a lifestyle offence under the Proceeds of Crime Act 2002 by paragraph 31 of Schedule 7 to this Act. The effect of this is that, where the court is considering making a confiscation order, it must assume that all the defendant's assets derive from his criminal conduct, unless he can prove otherwise. Because of the territorial restriction of the offence, it is not included in the list of Scheduled offences in Scotland.

Section 146: Section 145: supplementary

368. This section provides that the offence under section 145 applies to any act done in or out of any part of the United Kingdom. It creates extra-territorial effect as the provision applies to trafficking outside the United Kingdom when it is committed by specified categories of British national, and applies the forfeiture and detention provisions in respect of vehicles used to commit the offence which apply to the facilitation offences under the **new section 25** inserted by section 143. It also applies to a company incorporated anywhere in the United Kingdom. Section 163(2) provides that sections 145 and 146 extend only to England, Wales and Northern Ireland.

369. Subsection (4) provides that the trafficking offence shall be included in the schedule of offences against a child listed in Schedule 4 of the Criminal Justice and Court Services Act 2000. This means that those convicted of this offence against a person aged under 18 and who are sentenced to imprisonment or detention of twelve months or more will be disqualified from work with children

58

in the future, whether in a paid or unpaid capacity. Breach of such a disqualification order is a criminal offence.

370.   Schedule 7 adds an offence under section 145 to the list of Scheduled offences for the purposes of the Proceeds of Crime Act 2002. Because of the territorial restriction of the offence, it is not included in the list of Scheduled offences in Scotland.

Section 147: Employment

371.   Section 147 amends section 8 of the Asylum and Immigration Act 1996 "the 1996 Act") and modifies the existing law on illegal working. Under section 8 of the 1996 Act it is an offence to employ a person aged 16 or over who is subject to immigration control unless:

That person has current and valid permission to be in the United Kingdom and that permission does not prevent him or her from taking the job in question;

The person comes into a category where such employment is otherwise allowed (e.g. asylum-seekers who have been given permission to work, student nurses admitted under the terms of the Immigration Rules who may enter into contracts of employment without any additional permission being required).

372.   A statutory defence is provided in section 8(2) of the 1971 Act. The employer needs to prove that they have taken two steps in order to establish this defence. First, the employer must have had produced to him a document which appeared to him to relate to the worker in question and to be of a description specified in an order by the Secretary of State. The current order is the Immigration (Restrictions on Employment) Order 1996 SI 1996/3225. Second, the employer must have retained the document or a copy of it.

373.   Subsection (2) inserts two new subsections in the 1996 Act in place of section 8(2) of the 1996 Act. Under subsection (2) it will be a defence for a person charged with an offence under section 8 to prove that he complied with any relevant requirement of an order made by the Secretary of State under subsection (2A). Subsection (2A) expands the type of document that an employer could be required to see under such an order. In practice this could mean that, to establish a defence, an employer must demonstrate that he has seen two documents of particular types, and to produce copies of these when required.

374.   Subsection (4) provides new ancillary powers of entry, search and arrest in relation to the section 8 offence. Immigration officers will have powers of entry to arrest by warrant, entry and search of premises by warrant in order to obtain relevant evidence, entry and search of premises after arrest, search of arrested persons and search of persons in police custody.

Section 148: Registration Card

375.   Section 148 inserts section 26A into the 1971 Act which creates a number of new offences relating to the creation, possession and use of false or altered registration cards.

376.   Subsections (1) and (2) define a registration card as a card containing information about a person issued by the Secretary of State in connection with a claim for asylum. A "claim for asylum" is a claim made for asylum or for protection under Article 3 of the European Convention on Human Rights. A card may issued to the asylum claimant themselves or to a spouse or dependant of that claimant.

377.   The offences are contained in subsection (3). These include making a false card, altering a genuine card with intent to deceive (or to enable someone else to deceive), possessing a false or altered card without reasonable excuse, using a false card, and using an altered genuine card with intent to deceive. There are also offences relating to equipment designed to be used in making or altering cards.

378.   The maximum custodial sentence for the offences involving "possession" of a false or altered card or an article designed to make one is two years following conviction on indictment. The maximum custodial sentence for the other offences (including making, altering and using the card) is ten years imprisonment.

379.   Subsections (7) and (8) provide that the Secretary of State may amend the definition of a card by order.

Section 149: Immigration Stamp
380.   Section 149 creates an offence of possession of an immigration stamp, whether genuine or a replica, without a reasonable excuse. The offence relates to stamps used by immigration officers or officers acting on behalf of the Secretary of State to endorse documents, when exercising their powers under the Immigration Acts. It is punishable by a maximum custodial sentence of two years, a fine or both.

Section 150: Sections 148 and 149: consequential amendments
381.   This section contains ancillary powers in relation to the immigration stamp and registration card offences. Immigration officers or police constables can arrest someone suspected of having committed these offences without a warrant. They can also enter premises by warrant in order to search for and arrest a person suspected of committing one of these offences. Finally they can enter premises by warrant in order to search for evidence relevant to these offences.

Section 151: False information
382.   It is an offence (under section 26(1)(c) of the 1971 Act) to make a false return statement or representation to an immigration officer or other person lawfully acting in the execution of a relevant enactment. Section 151 amends the definition of relevant enactment to include the provisions contained in this Act (apart from Part 5).

Procedure
Section 152: Arrest by immigration officer

383. At present, the employment offence in section 8 of the Asylum and Immigration Act 1996 does not carry the power of arrest. To date the only way that it has been possible to make arrests by relying on police powers in the Police and Criminal Evidence Act 1984 ("PACE").

384. However, these powers only apply to constables and do not allow immigration officers to make arrests. Section 152 adds a separate power of arrest by warrant in relation to the section 8 offence. In addition, it remedies an anomaly in relation to offences under section 24(1)(d) of the Immigration Act 1971 – failure to comply with a requirement to report to, attend or submit to a medical examination. There is currently a power under section 28B of the 1971 Act to enter premises under a warrant in order to search for and arrest someone who is liable to be arrested for the section 24(1)(d) offence, but there is currently no free-standing power of arrest. Section 152 provides one.

Sections 153 and 154: Power of entry and to search for evidence

385. Section 153 gives immigration officers and police officers the power to enter business premises to search for, and, where appropriate, arrest immigration offenders where they have reasonable grounds for believing that such an offender is on the premises. Authorisation to use this power must be given by a senior officer (either an Assistant Director of Immigration or a Chief Superintendent of police) and is valid for a period of seven days beginning on the day it was given.

386. Section 154 gives immigration officers and police constables powers to search business premises without having to obtain a warrant if a person liable to arrest for an offence under section 24 or section 24(A) of the 1971 Act or paragraph 17 of Schedule 2 to that Act has been found on those premises, **and** the officer reasonably believes that an offence under section 8 of the 1996 Act has been committed and that there are employee records on the premises which are likely to be of substantial value in the investigation of the offence. These powers also allow the constable or immigration officer to seize records of value to the investigation of an immigration employment offence or an offence under section 105 or 106 of the 1999 Act. However, they do not allow items subject to legal privilege to be seized.

387. Separately, section154 also gives immigration officers a power to obtain a warrant in order to search business premises by warrant where the officer reasonably believes that the employer has provided inaccurate or incomplete information under the compulsory disclosure provisions of section 134 of this Act. Officers will be able to seize and retain employee records (other than items subject to legal privilege) where they suspect that they will be of substantial value to the investigation of an offence under section 137 of this act or under section 105 or 106 of the Immigration and Asylum Act 1999.

Section 156: Time limit on prosecution

388. Where an offence is triable only summarily, proceedings have to be brought within 6 months of the offence being committed unless the legislation provides for a longer period. Offences under section 24A and 25 of the 1971 Act will no longer be summary offences. Section 156 amends the sections of the 1971 Act which provide that an extended time limit shall apply in respect of those offences accordingly.

PART 8: GENERAL

Section 157: Consequential and incidental provision

389. This section provides a power for the Secretary of State to make amendments to other legislation, in limited circumstances, namely that the amendments are consequential or incidental to a provision in this Act.

390. Subsection (4) makes it clear that an order, by which another enactment is amended, can only be made if it is approved by both Houses of Parliament.

391. Subsection (5) provides that where an order does anything else, it can be made provided that no contrary view is expressed by either House

Section 161: Repeals

392. Section 161 introduces Schedule 9 which sets out the extent to which current immigration, nationality and race relations legislation is repealed by the provisions of this Act.

COMMENCEMENT

393. Section 162 contains provisions relating to the coming into force of the Act. Subsection (2) provides for the specified provisions to come into force on the passing of this Act. The remaining provisions come into force on such dates as the Secretary of State by order appoints.

HANSARD REFERENCES

394. The following table sets out the dates and Hansard references for each stage of the Act's passage through Parliament.

Stage	Date	Hansard Reference

HOUSE OF COMMONS		
Introduction and First Reading	12 April 2002	Vol 383 Col 263
Second Reading	24 April 2002	Vol 384 Cols 341-436
Standing Committee	10 sittings between 30 April and 21 May 2002	
	30 April 2002	1st sitting Cols 1-64
	7 May 2002	2nd sitting Cols 65-104
	9 May 2002	3rd sitting Cols 105–138
	9 May 2002	4th sitting Cols 139-192
	14 May 2002	5th sitting Cols 193-232
	14 May 2002	6th sitting Cols 233-278
	16 May 2002	7th sitting Cols 279-310
	16 May 2002	8th sitting Cols 311-362
	21 May 2002	9th sitting Cols 363-396
	21 May 2002	10th sitting Cols 397-460
Report Stage	11 June 2002	Vol 386 Cols 727-838
Report and Third Reading	12 June 2002	Vol 386 Cols 870-967
HOUSE OF LORDS		
Introduction	13 June 2002	Vol 636 Col 390
2nd Reading	24 June 2002	Vol 636 Cols 1087-1181

Committee Stage	8 July 2002, 9 July 2002, 10 July 2002, 15 July 2002 and 17 July 2002. 23 July 2002 and 29 July 2002	Vol 637, Cols 440-554,565-678,689-814, 963-1084 and 1233-1388. Vol 638 Cols 261-360 and 676-738
Report Stage	9 October 2002 10 October 2002	Vol 639 Cols 263-400 * Vol 639 Cols 411-550
Re-commitment	17 October 2002	Vol 639 Cols 974-1057
Report Stage	24 October 2002	Vol 639 Cols 1436-1558
Third Reading	31 October 2002	Vol 640 Cols 292-421
Commons Consideration of Lords Amendments	5 November 2002	Vol 392 Cols 145-244
Lords Consideration of Commons Amendments.	6 November 2002	Vol 640 Cols 758-856
Commons Consideration of Lords Amendments	7 November 2002	Vol 392 Cols 452-471
Lords Consideration of Commons Amendments.	7 November 2002	Vol 640 Cols 942-948
ROYAL ASSENT	7 November 2002	Vol 392 Col 480

Printed in the UK by The Stationery Office Limited
under the authority and superintendence of Carol Tullo, Controller of
Her Majesty's Stationery Office and Queen's Printer of Acts of Parliament